DISCOVER HOW REAL-LIFE MEN AND WOMEN FOUND THE ULTIMATE IN SEXUAL PLEASURE . . .

♥ It starts out as an impulsive trip to a porno movie theater for forty-one-year-old Sheila and her husband, but what is happening on the screen isn't half as hot as what Sheila is going to do in the back row . . .

♥ A Las Vegas weekend turns very naughty when Harriet and her husband Randy invite a gorgeous call girl to their room for an experience that proves that two is company, but three is ecstasy.

♥ Sukie, a twenty-three-year-old nurse, keeps hearing about her best friend's fabulous lover—until she finds herself alone with him, and succumbing to an irresistible urge to make love, even though the odds are they may get caught.

♥ Ellen and Chuck, young marrieds with two small children, never seem to have time for good sex, until they go off on a getaway weekend alone with the plans—and the sex toys—to make their most forbidden, outrageous fantasies come true . . .

NOTHING THAT GIVES FULFILLMENT AND PLEASURE IS TABOO AND EVERYTHING IS FILLED WITH THE SPECIAL EXCITEMENT OF . . .

THE BEST SEX I EVER HAD

The Best
SEX
I Ever Had!

REAL PEOPLE RECALL
THEIR MOST EROTIC
EXPERIENCES

Steven and Iris Finz

ST. MARTIN'S PAPERBACKS

THE BEST SEX I EVER HAD

Copyright © 1992 by Steven and Iris Finz.

All rights reserved. No part of this book may be used or reproduced in any manner whatsoever without written permission except in the case of brief quotations embodied in critical articles or reviews. For information address St. Martin's Press, 175 Fifth Avenue, New York, N.Y. 10010.

Library of Congress Catalog Card Number: 92-848

ISBN: 0-312-95083-7

Printed in the United States of America

St. Martin's Press hardcover edition / June 1992
St. Martin's Paperbacks edition / August 1993

10 9 8 7 6 5 4 3

To our readers.

May this book help you to
achieve the best sex you
ever had.

CONTENTS

INTRODUCTION

THE BEST SEX
YOU'LL EVER HAVE

Most of us are hedonists at heart, putting our pleasures before our obligations. Left to our own designs, we would probably never do anything unpleasant unless forced to by our personal needs. So Nature made sex feel good as part of a wonderful scheme to guarantee that as humans grow old and eventually die, they will be replaced by offspring.

To have two or three children, a couple must ordinarily engage in sexual intercourse many more than two or three times. To assure that this will happen, nature made the physical sensations connected with sex so intensely enjoyable that, once experienced, they can never be put completely out of mind. As a result, few of us think about reproduction while we are making love. Instead, we concentrate on the pleasure of our erotic contacts. In doing so, we are carrying out Nature's plan.

No one needs instruction in the mechanics of copulation. Even the clumsy coupling of inexperienced adolescents is sufficient to get the job done and pleasurable enough to bring them back for more. As we mature and acquire sophistication, however, we seek ways to refine our enjoyment.

People who like sex are always looking for ways to

make good sex better. They explore their own minds, seeking new ideas or attempting to put new twists on the old ones. They experiment with their partners in an effort to find techniques that will increase their gratification and intensify their sensations. Some even study human sexuality to learn why certain acts feel better than others.

We recently wrote a book entitled *Whispered Secrets** about the erotic fantasies that couples share in whispers during their most intimate moments. While gathering material for it, we asked dozens of couples to tell us about their favorite erotic fantasies. Frequently, instead of telling us about their fantasies, the couples we interviewed described real experiences. They said that these experiences were so intense that they were better than even their wildest fantasies.

As we collected their stories, we found ourselves learning about our own sexuality. Most of the things that turned other people on turned us on also. We began experimenting with activities that led other couples to what they called the best sex they ever had. In doing so, we found that our sex, which has always been good, was getting even better.

Researchers like Masters and Johnson or Alfred Kinsey and his associates also induced their subjects to be frank and candid about their sexuality. When they wrote about their findings, however, they clinicized and conceptualized until the behavior they studied lost its erotic quality. Their works may teach us about human nature, but rarely help us to improve our own sex lives.

The approach that this book takes is much more direct. Without attempting to analyze or explain the

*Iris and Steven Finz, *Whispered Secrets: The Couple's Guide to Erotic Fantasy*. New York: Signet, 1990.

reasons for it, we recount the experiences that our subjects found to be their sexiest. We present their stories with very little editing so that those who read them can gain personally and informally.

There are two ways to use this book to make your own sex more satisfying. The simplest is by turning the erotic experiences of others into a kind of aphrodisiac or sexual stimulant. In the chapter entitled "Seeing and Being Seen," several people mention a special excitement that comes from watching others make love. To some extent, this tendency, called "voyeurism," is present in each of us.

Reading the descriptions of experiences that the participants regard as their best sex ever is a little like peeking into their bedrooms with their permission. By doing so, you can indulge your own streak of voyeurism. Sharing these accounts with your partner (by reading your favorite passages aloud, for example) may carry you both to soaring heights of excitement, moving you to explore more deeply your own sensuality and discover new ways of stimulating each other. This cannot help but lead to better sex.

The other way of deriving benefit from this anthology of erotic recollections is to regard it as a book of suggestions, a menu of sexuality. You may find that some of the stories are about things you've thought of doing but never actually have. Perhaps you are too embarrassed to tell your mate what you are thinking. Maybe you believe that the idea is too unusual for anyone else to understand. Seeing it in print may help you realize that you are not alone in your desire, that your fantasy is not a perversion.

On the other hand, some of the stories may give you ideas that you never had before. It might not have occurred to you, for example, that agreeing to refrain from sex for a specified period of time would add a special fillip to your relationship. You might never have considered pretending to be an armed assailant or a hooker from an escort service. The thought of offering yourself to your spouse as an erotic surprise or as a personal sex slave for the weekend might be a new and exciting one for you. Reading about an act that inflames or excites two strangers may make you want to experiment with it yourself.

Nobody has a copyright on sexual activities. If you find one that you think you might like, it's yours to try. When you read a story that you enjoy, sit back and think about it for a while. Close your eyes and visualize yourself and your mate in a similar situation. If it still seems exciting, show the story to your partner, and if she or he is willing, go ahead and do it. (Remember, though, that casual sex can be deadly unless the proper precautions are taken.)

The fact that you have bought this book indicates that you are attuned to your own erotic nature. You may think that your sex is already as good as it will ever get, but this can never be true. No matter how terrific your relationship is, there will always be room for it to get better. We hope the stories in this book will help to show you how.

1

FORBIDDEN FRUIT

Every society has a cosmogony, a theory about how the universe came into being. The ancient Greeks attributed creation to a game played by mischievous gods who resided on a holy mountain called Olympus. Some Eastern peoples believe that the Eternal Being imagined the Earth and everything on it so He would have something to love. Most of Western civilization looks to the explanation contained in Genesis, the first book of the Old Testament.

According to that story, the Creator fashioned a wonderful garden with rivers running cool and clear and an abundance of everything necessary for human comfort. All that the first pair of Homo sapiens needed to do was be fruitful and multiply, while enjoying the produce that dangled from every tree. Every tree but one, that is, for there was one fruit that they were forbidden to sample. This, of course, was the one that they found irresistible. Eating it cost them dearly, but eat it they did.

There are those who say that Genesis is a factually accurate account of the beginning of the world. Others call it poetry, insisting that its images attempt to express symbolically an infinite truth that cannot be communicated directly. None can doubt, however, that the Judaic-Christian cosmogony, like that of any other culture, reflects an understanding of human nature.

Adam and Eve's fall from grace illustrates a fact about people in our society. Whatever the risk, whatever the price, if a fruit is forbidden to us, we must taste it. After we do, we are likely to declare that forbidden fruit is the sweetest.

For many people, this is especially true of sexuality. Resenting the rules that regulate their lives and that are usually created by others, these people seek opportunities to flout accepted standards of propriety. Often, this leads them to experiment with sexual partners or sexual behaviors of which they have been taught to think as forbidden or taboo. The incidents described in this chapter were recounted by people who claim to have had their most exciting erotic experiences while violating the rules that they were brought up to obey.

TEMPTING FATE

S_ukie, twenty-three, has cur-_
ly black hair and hazel eyes. She is of medium height with
what television commercials refer to as a "full figure"—
fleshy enough to be sexy without being considered fat. Her
heavy breasts fill the front of her crisp white nurse's uniform,
but her waist is comparatively trim. Sukie dates but has no
steady boyfriend at the moment. When asked to describe her
most erotic experience, she recalled a brief encounter that
she had one afternoon, saying that the possibility of getting
caught made it the best sex she can remember.

♥   ♥   ♥

I've always been proud of
my boobs. They're big and soft, exactly the kind that
most men like. In a way, these tits got me into the
situation I'm telling you about. They were the first
thing Jim mentioned when he got serious about putting the moves on me. But I'm getting ahead of myself.
Let me start at the beginning.

I'm not exactly what you'd call conservative, but I
don't usually do things like this. I guess it was about
the naughtiest thing I've ever done. I suppose I should
feel guilty about it, but to tell you the truth, I don't.
Not in the least. It was too exciting. I think the fact
that it was so naughty is what made it so exciting.

You know what they say, "Forbidden fruit tastes the sweetest."

My curiosity had been building for months, and it was really Gayle's fault. To some extent, the blame is hers. She was so open and so very explicit about her relationship with Jim. She practically bragged about it, telling me all the intimate details of their private sex life. It was "Jim this" and "Jim that" every time I saw her.

I'm a nurse, you know, and Gayle is, too. She's about the same age as I am. We work at the same hospital and see each other almost every day. You might say she's my best friend. That's one of the things that makes this all so weird.

Well, about six months ago, Gayle got involved with Jim. He plays in a local rock-and-roll band. Gayle moved in with him after just a couple of dates. When she told me about it, she said that she wasn't really in love with him, but that their sex was so great that it was enough for her. She said that he was the best lover she ever had. Oh, I mean she positively raved about him.

She told me that he could make love to her for hours, giving her one orgasm after another without coming himself and without ever going soft. She said that he had an immense dick and that when he put it in her she felt totally filled. She went into intricate detail, telling me about the positions they used, about the dirty things he whispered in her ear while they were screwing, about the way he licked her clit, even about how he put the tip of his finger in her ass.

Every time we had one of those conversations, I found myself getting turned on. One afternoon she spent an entire lunch hour describing the things they had done the night before. By the time she was done, I was horny, I was frustrated, and I felt like I would jump the first guy that came my way. Finally, I ended up going to the ladies' room and doing myself just to relieve the tension.

Almost every day, Gayle would tell me pornographic stories about her and Jim. I think she got a kick out of getting me all worked up with her descriptions. She was making me feel envious of her superactive sex life, and I think she knew it. There were times I felt like telling her to keep the details to herself, but I couldn't really bring myself to say that. The truth is, I guess I liked hearing it as much as she liked telling it.

When she asked me to come by to meet him one evening, I jumped at the chance. I was dying of curiosity. I couldn't wait to see her superman with my own eyes. I guess I was expecting some kind of Greek god. Well, he was far from it.

Jim turned out to be short and on the slight side, with long brown hair tied back into a ponytail. His eyes were set deep into his face, giving him the look of a thinker. His teeth were a little crooked, but he had an easy smile and an extremely charming manner. When we first met, he greeted me like an old friend, acting as if he'd known me all his life.

By the flirtatious expression he wore and the intimate way he touched my hand or shoulder as he spoke to me, I could tell that he was really into sex. I couldn't help liking him right from the start. Through it all, there was an undercurrent of sexual curiosity. Every time I looked at him, I imagined all the things Gayle told me about him. When he moved, his jeans drew tight across his crotch, and I remembered what Gayle had said about the size of his dick.

It was obvious that he liked talking about sex. No matter what the topic of conversation was, Jim managed to connect it to something erotic. When I said that I needed to go on a diet, he looked directly at my boobs and said, "Just be careful not to lose any weight in those gorgeous tits of yours." When I said something about the food Gayle was serving, he said, "Food isn't the only thing worth eating." He even managed to make his smile appear lewd and suggestive, something about the way he raised one bushy eyebrow and licked his lips with the darting tip of his tongue.

After Gayle had been living with him for a while, I started dropping in regularly to join them for dinner or to watch a show with them on TV. Jim always flirted with me, but in a way that wasn't threatening or annoying. Actually, I liked it. It made me feel attractive. Gayle didn't seem to mind at all. I think she was proud of the fact that she had such a sexy boyfriend. As long as he didn't actually fool around, she didn't object to a little flirtation.

One Saturday, I was working at the hospital when I got a call from Gayle. She had the day off. "Why don't you come over for lunch?" she said. "We're only a couple of blocks away, and you can probably stretch your lunch hour to ninety minutes. If you call me just before you leave, I'll have everything ready."

She was right about my being able to steal a little extra time for lunch. It was Saturday, and I knew no one would notice. "Sure," I said. "Sounds good to me." I swear it was all perfectly innocent. I had no idea of what was about to happen. None at all.

I phoned Gayle at about one o'clock to say that I was on my way. I briefed the other nurses about my problem patients so that everything would be taken care of while I was out. Then I headed for Gayle and Jim's.

When I knocked on the door, Jim answered it. "Hi, sexy," he said, squashing my tits against his chest as he grabbed me in a warm bear hug. "Did you see Gayle when you were coming in?"

"No," I answered. "Where is she?"

"She had to go to the hospital," he said. "Nursing supervisor called her. Some kind of emergency. She said she'd be back real soon, though."

"That's a fine thing," I joked. "She invites me over for lunch and then runs out on me. Now I suppose I'll starve."

"Worry not," he answered, his eyes taking on that flirtatious twinkle. "I've got something you can eat." With both hands, he framed the snug crotch of his jeans, pulling the worn fabric tight against his bulge.

When he did that, I couldn't help picturing his genitals. It wasn't my fault; it was Gayle's. She was always telling me that he had the biggest dick in the world. It was only natural for me to fantasize about it. Just because we see lots of them, don't think that nurses aren't interested in men's sex organs. We're human too, you know.

I felt the involuntary sexual thoughts reddening my face. It was embarrassing, especially because I knew that it revealed what I was thinking. I wanted to turn away but couldn't do so gracefully.

Jim noticed, of course. "Are you getting turned on?" he asked with a grin. "Don't try to deny it. I can see those nipple hard-ons right through your uniform. You've got gorgeous tits; anyone can see that. I'll bet your nipples are something else. Do you know how many hours I've spent imagining what it would be like to touch them?"

I didn't know what to say. I just felt my ears getting hotter and hotter. My nipples responded to his words, becoming so hard with excitement that they ached.

He took a step closer. "Why don't you show them to me?" he said. "Just one little look, that's all. Now that won't do any harm, will it?" As he spoke, he placed his hand on my shoulder. With a slowness that was almost painful, he trailed slowly downward until he was caressing one of my breasts through the white fabric. His touch was so light and soft that for a moment I wasn't sure he was making any contact at all. But when he traced a little circle around my erect nipple with his fingertip, there was no doubt about it. "Just one little look," he repeated in a soft whisper.

Without waiting for my answer, he deftly undid two of my buttons. I just stood there letting him. I was actually trembling, like a girl getting felt up for the first time. I can't remember a man's touch ever feeling that good before. My inaction increased his confidence, and he opened another button, exposing the laciness of my plunge bra. I was too nervous to look down, but I knew that the fullness of my breasts overflowed the demicups, creating a deep and sensuous cleavage. I could almost feel the weight of his gaze as he stared at my bosom.

"Magnificent," he murmured, opening the rest of my buttons. Without a word, I stepped out of the dress, standing before him in bra and half-slip. He had me out of the slip so fast that I still don't know how he accomplished it. My bra and panties were brief and white, made of lace to match the bands at the tops of the thigh-high stockings that I wore instead of pantyhose.

He took a step back and examined me for a long time with his eyes. His study was slow, patient, and unashamed. The way he looked at each part of me, nodding his head and murmuring with approval, made me feel like the most desirable woman on earth. He even walked around me in a slow circle, caressing me with the frankness of his gaze.

10

When he finally reached for the snap of my bra, I was so aroused that I would have done anything he wanted. He asked nothing of me, so I just stood there letting him enjoy me with his eyes and fingertips. He removed the bra lovingly, stroking my back and shoulders with hands that were hungry but unhurried. My pebble-hard nipples craved his seductive touch, but it seemed like forever before he got to them.

First he traced the outer curves of my breasts, bringing tingling gooseflesh to my white skin. Then he ran his fingertips lightly over my abdomen, coming close to the bottoms of my boobs but not actually touching them. Finally, he cupped my breasts gently, holding one in each of his strong hands but not squeezing or abusing them. I could feel my legs beginning to shake.

Somewhere inside, I realized that he was my best friend's boyfriend and that she might return to catch us at any minute. But instead of making me want to quit, that thought only made me more excited. I kept telling myself, "Just one more minute. Just one more minute."

At last, Jim took my nipples between his thumbs and forefingers, rolling them lightly to increase their erection. I was tingling from head to toe as he thrilled me with his erotic expertise. "I've been wanting to hold them for so long," he whispered, his breath tickling my ear.

I could feel the crotch of my panties become wet as I thought of his dick. I wanted to see it but was powerless to do anything other than submit to his skill. His thumbs hooked the waistband of my white lace briefs, lowering them just the slightest fraction of an inch. Although they still covered me, I felt as naked as Eve. I wanted him to see all of me. I wanted to show him my most intimate parts, to give him access to my most secret places.

A millimeter at a time, he lowered the undergarment, caressing my hips with his fingers as he did so. Now a narrow band of curling black hair was showing above the elastic. Now the entire expanse of my mound was uncovered. Finally, nothing but the damp crotch of the lacy wisp remained in contact with my body, connected to me by the wetness that made it cling to my vaginal membranes. A moment later, I was naked except for my stockings.

He took me into his arms again, his hands roaming freely over my nude body. I felt him exploring the dark crevice that separated my buttocks and slipping the tip of his finger between the lips of my vulva. My heart was beating a mile a minute.

I reached clumsily for his bulge but couldn't get my hand between our bodies. Sensing my desire, he stepped back. "Here," he said, undoing the buttons of his fly. "I'll make it easier for you." Opening his jeans, he shoved them down over his narrow hips and stepped out of them. He wore no underwear, and his massive dick sprang forward unfettered. I've never seen a bigger one. It was huge, every bit as big as Gayle told me it was.

At the sudden memory of Gayle, I became frightened. She could be back at any minute. What was I doing with her boyfriend, naked and staring at his cock? I knew I should get dressed and get out of there. But I knew that I couldn't. There was just no way.

I reached out to take that mammoth tool in my hand, feeling its warmth with my fingers. It was throbbing, like a creature with its own heartbeat. Shuddering involuntarily with pleasure at the thought, I imagined how it would feel to have such a large cock inside me.

"Come with me," he said softly. "I want to fuck you. Now. Before Gayle gets back." With one hand, he scooped up the clothes that lay strewn about the floor. With the other, he took my elbow and directed me toward the bedroom. Without thinking, guided only by my sexual appetite, I let him lead me where he would.

The bed was unmade, and I imagined Jim and Gayle fucking on it only a few hours earlier. The mental picture excited me even more. Perversely, I wanted him to screw me in the same place he screwed her. I was terrified that Gayle would walk in on us, but somehow the possibility of that excited me, too.

Wordlessly, he led me to the bed and eased me down onto my back. I looked at him, waiting to see what he would do next. I felt totally submissive, completely at his command. He stood there for a moment, looking hungrily at me and stroking his gigantic erection with his hand. "We don't have much time," he said.

Then, almost before I realized what was happening, he was on the bed, poised on his knees between my parted thighs. There was nothing between his cock and my pussy but air, and not much of that. He moved closer, until he was touching my labia with his dick. Holding the organ in his hand, he moved it up and down wetting it thoroughly with the oozing juices of my desire.

"I'm going to fuck you now," he said. "And I won't stop until you come." He moved forward, inserting the head of his hard-on in my vulva. "Do you understand?"

I nodded dumbly, feeling his huge cock sliding in and in and in. When I thought my pussy wouldn't take any more, he slid it in even farther. The hugeness of it filled me. At last I felt the hardness of his pubis bumping against my mound and I knew that he was buried completely.

The knowledge that I was fucking Jim in Gayle's bed filled me with a sense of danger. But his promise to make me come pushed all other thoughts out of my mind. I wanted it. That was all I knew. I wanted it bad.

He moved as if we had all the time in the world, sliding his cock almost all the way out of me before reversing direction to push it in again. Its thickness had my vaginal membranes stretched as far as they could go, but the tightness of the fit increased the friction, making the pleasure of his thrusts even more intense. When he sank to the depths inside my vagina, I could feel the hairs of his scrotum caressing the skin of my ass. I rocked up against him, crying out involuntarily as the pleasure overwhelmed me.

He increased the tempo of his movements slightly, knowing instinctively what it took to please me. Each time he drove inside, his almost hairless chest brushed the tips of my erect nipples, sending tingling bolts of energy from my breasts to the heart of my pussy.

He was fucking me steadily now, without stopping between strokes. It was impossible to tell where the outstroke ended and the instroke began. It seemed to go on forever. His ability to keep up the steady pace without slowing and without reaching his own peak made him the perfect sex partner.

I groaned as I felt my climax approaching. I knew that once it started I would be helpless. I knew that for an erotic eternity the orgasm would dominate my spirit, that all thought would be banished. The fear that Gayle might walk in at any moment was still present, but it was not an effective force in directing my behavior. I felt like a single unitary sex organ, doing what I had been created to do.

14

Unaware that anything existed except the ecstasy of sensation, I sobbed as the waves of release began to break. Through it all, Jim kept up the steady pounding of his dick inside my body. He drove it in and out in perfect harmony with the melody played by the bliss of my wanton orgasm. For that long interminable moment, I felt it would never end. Then I reached the peak and began the long slide back to reality.

The falling action was almost complete when I heard a sound that made my blood freeze in my veins. It was the unmistakable scraping of a key being fitted into a lock. Jim heard it, too.

"Gayle's home," he whispered. "Have you had enough?" Even now, he continued stroking my core with his erection. "Did I keep my promise?"

"Oh, God, yes," I answered, choking with panic. "I don't want her to catch us. Oh, please."

Calmly, showing no real sign of fear, Jim rolled off me and rose to his feet. Almost as if it were an everyday experience for him, he quickly and efficiently gathered my clothes and presented them to me, pointing me toward the bathroom. As I ran, I saw him step casually into his jeans and button the front.

Through the bathroom door, I heard him greeting Gayle warmly in the same sexy tone he had used while undressing me. I rushed into my clothes and flushed the toilet. When I came out, Gayle and Jim were locked in a passionate embrace that made it obvious that they would be fucking just minutes after I left. The thought that his cock would still be covered with my juices gave me a kind of perverse pleasure that I still don't understand.

Looking at my watch, I said, "Well, Gayle, my lunch hour's over and I've got to head back. Thanks for lunch."

"Sorry," she said. "I'll have to make it up to you."

"That won't be necessary," I answered, looking right into Jim's twinkling eyes. "I'm not really complaining."

I thought I saw him smile, but Gayle didn't even seem to hear me. She wasn't paying attention to me, clearly eager to get her boyfriend into bed as soon as possible. I accommodated her by leaving at once.

I'm still friendly with Gayle and I still go to their apartment all the time, but I never did it with Jim again. I wouldn't want to do anything to interfere with their relationship, even though I am a little envious. I'll never forget that afternoon, though, when my best friend's boyfriend gave me the best sex I ever had.

HIGHER EDUCATION

J*erry, twenty years old, is just under six feet tall and has the lean sinewy body of a long-distance runner. His fair complexion gives him a clean-cut all-American look. He keeps his dusty-blond hair short to decrease wind resistance. Jerry lives to run. He is a star on the track team at a small university. Not long ago, his athletic scholarship was in jeopardy when his grades fell. His piercing blue eyes flash as he tells about how that incident led to the best sex he ever had.*

♥   ♥   ♥

To me, the most important thing about college is the track team. I know it doesn't sound very academic, but let's face it, I'm not really an academic guy. I've been a runner ever since I can remember. When I was a little kid, I would run miles and miles for the thrill of it. In high school, I joined the track team just for fun. It never occurred to me that running might pay off in some way.

By the time I was a junior, I started getting letters from colleges, making me all kinds of offers. I never planned to go to college, but I jumped at the chance to continue running and not have to think about finding a job. Now I'm pretty close to graduating from college and I still haven't started thinking about a job. Coach

17

says there's a living to be made in long-distance running, but not much of one. My dad says it's a shame I didn't pick baseball or basketball or football. Now, that's where the money is. But I don't care. Running is my life.

About a year ago, it started to look like I was going to lose everything. I've never been much of a student. Let's face it, I never wanted to be. I'm no brain. No matter how hard I study, I still come out with lousy grades. Coach always says not to worry about it as long as I maintain the mandatory C grade average. For my first couple of quarters, I did keep a C average, even though it was by the skin of my teeth.

Then I took math to complete my general-ed requirements, and that was almost the end of the line. I really tried. I even got a tutor. But I just couldn't cut it. Oh, I can add and subtract, but when it comes to algebra and geometry, there's just nothing I can do. It's like a foreign language to me.

I flunked it the first time, and they said I'd have to take it again. So I did, but it looked like I was heading for a second F. I knew it was hopeless. The trouble was that all my other grades were borderline, and flunking math again would pull me down below the C average I needed to stay on the team. I went to Coach and told him the problem, but he just said that if I worked a little harder everything would be all right.

I didn't know what I was going to do. Then on top of all that, I get this letter from Dean Smith telling me to make an appointment to see her as soon as possible. I was scared shitless that she was going to kick me out.

When I went to her office, I was real nervous. But she turned out to be a very nice lady. Even though I never met her before, she greeted me like an old friend. "Hi, Jerry," she said. "You sure have turned our track team around."

"Thank you, Dean," I mumbled. Man, was I uncomfortable about being there.

"Sit down, please," she invited, gesturing to one of her guest chairs.

"Am I in some trouble, ma'am?" I asked, perching nervously in the seat.

Dean Smith's warm, feminine laugh made me take a good look at her for the first time. She was maybe fifty years old, but she must really have been a knockout when she was young. For a woman her age, she was still very attractive.

She had short blond hair and great blue eyes that kind of sparkled when she smiled. The thing I noticed most was her body. She was curvy in all the right places, and firm, like she took good care of herself. She had real nice tits and a terrific ass, and wore clothes that showed it. Her tight-fitting skirt hugged those buns, and her low-cut silk blouse showed enough cleavage to be distracting. When I caught myself studying her figure, I quickly looked away. The last thing I needed right then was to piss the dean off.

"You're not in trouble yet," she said. Her voice was kind of husky and sexy. "But you've got to pass math. Coach Riley is a good friend of mine. He tells me our track team hasn't been this good in twenty years, which, for a lot of reasons, is wonderful for the school. The coach says he can't afford to lose you. So I promised I'd try to help you through it."

I looked at her in confusion.

"I used to be a math teacher, you know," she said with a trace of pride. "In fact, I was chair of the math department before I became dean."

I couldn't figure out what she was getting at until she held a package of worksheets out to me and said,

"I want you to do your best with the problems in Chapter One of this study packet. Then come back to see me on Thursday right after track practice. And bring the problems with you."

I couldn't believe it. The dean was going to tutor me in math. None of my teammates could believe it, either. It just didn't make sense. Artie, a senior on the team, had a theory. "I've heard rumors that the dean likes to screw young jocks," he said. "Maybe she just wants to get into your pants." Everybody in the locker room laughed and hooted when he said it. The idea was just so ridiculous.

I worked on the math problems and went back to see her on Thursday as she instructed. Her secretary kept me waiting in the outer office for a minute. Then the dean came to get me herself. She led me to her office and gestured toward the couch, closing the door behind us. "Sit down," she said.

She was wearing a dress with a wide skirt and a plunging neckline. When she sat down on the couch beside me, she crossed her legs carelessly, causing the skirt to ride high enough to give me a long view of her shapely thighs. For a dean, she was one good-looking woman.

As she slid closer to me, I was aware of the scent of her perfume and the warmth of her leg against mine. "Where are the worksheets I gave you?" she asked. She seemed to be looking into my eyes in a very un-deanlike manner. I got a little flustered.

"I've got them right here," I answered, patting all my pockets before realizing that I was holding them in my hand. "Uh, right here, I mean." I spread the papers out in my lap.

She laughed musically, touching my shoulder lightly. "Don't be nervous," she said. "This won't hurt a bit. Now, let's see what you've got here." She took one of the sheets from my lap and held it up in front of her face. "Hmmm," she murmured, studying my work. "This doesn't look *totally* hopeless." She put the worksheet back on my lap, her hand accidentally brushing across my bare thigh. My skin tingled where she had touched me.

I've had some experience with sex. I mean, you know how the girls like athletes. I've had my share. But there was something especially sexy about this fifty-year-old woman. Maybe it was the fact that she was the dean of the college, which made her just about as off-limits as a person can be. I don't know. Whatever the reason, I realized that I was getting a little turned on just sitting next to her on the couch. When she had touched my leg, my cock stirred. I hoped she hadn't noticed.

"One mistake you're making is that you keep inverting the equations," she said. Or some such bullshit. The truth is I'm not really sure what the hell she was saying, because as she said it, she was pointing to my mistakes on the worksheet resting in my lap.

Each time she tapped her manicured finger against the paper, I felt an electric shock go straight through to my dick, which was right under it. She kept touching the paper to make her point, and I was starting to get embarrassingly stiff. I wanted to move the worksheet away before I got busted, but if I had, my hard-on would have been obvious.

Now she started underlining the equations on the worksheet with her fingertip, drawing imaginary circles around the numbers. Although I was sure she didn't mean to, she was tickling and stroking my cock. It felt good, even though I was dying of fright. It never occurred to me that she was doing it on purpose.

21

I noticed that her other hand seemed to be fidgeting with the buttons at the front of her dress, opening and closing them without even seeming to know it. Each time she undid one of the buttons, I got a little glimpse of the smooth white skin of her titties. I hoped I wasn't staring, but I just couldn't look away. When she suddenly took her hand from the buttons, I was sure I'd been busted. Then, to my surprise, she moved her hand to my leg and rested it lightly on my thigh where it was bare below the hem of my shorts.

I was beginning to wonder whether or not she was conscious of what she was doing. She kept talking about the math problems, but her words were totally meaningless to me. As she droned on, the hand that touched my leg seemed to move slightly. At the same moment, she laid her other hand flat on the worksheet to emphasize some point she was making. By now, my cock was at full erection.

"Dean Smith," I started, thinking I had to find some excuse to break away from there before I got myself in big trouble.

She looked right into my eyes. "Yes, Jerry?" she almost cooed. She was openly stroking my leg now, her fingers running lightly up and down the inside of my thigh and stopping every now and then to give it a gentle squeeze. "Do you like the way this feels?"

I couldn't say anything, but my cock started pulsating uncontrollably. With a swift movement of her hand, she pushed the worksheets from my lap, exposing the front of my shorts where my boner was straining against it. I thought I heard a soft sigh whisk from her throat.

"Nice," she murmured, closing her hand over the fabric. Her other hand slid boldly inside the leg of my shorts, her fingertips creeping closer and closer to the bulge my nuts made in the jock I was wearing. Involuntarily, I leaned back against the couch and closed my eyes.

I was scared to death, but I couldn't help surrendering to the wonderful sensations she was giving me with her talented touch. The dean! The dean of the whole fucking college! Here I was on her couch while she rubbed my cock and balls like a horny young co-ed. I didn't know what to make of it. I decided to just ride with the wave.

"I'll bet you've got a great big strong young cock," she whispered. "I want to see it." Her fingers worked at the waistband of my shorts, dragging them down along with my jock. I helped her a little by lifting my ass off the couch. The next thing I knew, she tossed them to the floor with the worksheets.

My cock was free now, standing up like a flagpole. I could feel her hungry eyes devouring it while her hands worked eagerly to make it even harder and stiffer. She circled the shaft of my pecker lightly with her thumb and fingers, stroking gently up toward the head and down against the hairy jungle at the base. Her other hand cupped and cradled my balls, treating them like valuable jewels.

She might have been a math teacher and she might have been a dean, but she could have taught a great class in Handjob 101. I've had quite a few girls pull my dick, but none with the style and skill of that middle-aged lady. Maybe it comes with experience.

She seemed to know all the places where a cock was especially sensitive. Those she didn't already know about, she discovered. Her hands were soft and loving, her fingers gliding over the smooth skin of my shaft. She obviously liked what she was doing. Her eyes were glazed and half closed. A seductive smile played around her lips. Her touch sent chills up my spine. It felt like I died and went to heaven.

From the corner of my eye, I happened to see her nameplate on the edge of her desk. It reminded me of where I was and who I was with. I knew that I was playing with fire, but desire had me by the balls, and as always, it was lust over logic. Besides, in a way it was probably the danger of the situation that made it so exciting. Can you imagine what would happen to a bonehead who got caught with his pants down in the dean's office?

She continued stroking my cock and balls with one hand, while the other slowly unbuttoned the front of her dress and unhooked her black lace bra. When it opened, her tits popped into view. They were medium-sized and pointed, with nipples so dark they were practically brown. I wanted to touch them, but I didn't know if that was allowed. She must have sensed my indecision, because she took my hand in hers and placed it on her tits. Then she went back to rubbing and stroking me.

When I got those boobs in my hands, I almost forgot whose tits I was feeling. They were as firm as a cheerleader's. I cupped them and stroked them and rolled the erect nipples between my fingers, making her groan with pleasure.

All the time, I was praying silently that her door was locked. If it wasn't, I hoped nobody would hear the sounds she was making and come in to investigate. This was probably the craziest thing I ever did. But all I could think about was how good it felt. Her hands playing with my cock and my fingers twirling her nipples were sending waves of excited pleasure through both of us at the same time. The thought of who she was and where we were doing it was making me even hotter.

24

Pressing gently against the back of my head, she pushed my face into the soft flesh of her bosom. At first, I just kept it there, holding her tits against it and inhaling deeply to smell the sweet perfume of her cleavage. Grabbing my hair, she moved my face until one of her brown nipples was pressed against my lips. It didn't take me long to get the point. I started sucking and nibbling it, hearing her moans reverberate against the walls of her office.

When I had thoroughly mouthed both of her titties, she pulled back and rose to her feet. I looked up in horror, certain that she had finally regained her senses and was about to call the campus police to have me locked up and the key melted down. Instead, she took a few shuffling steps backward toward her desk, keeping her eyes fastened on my throbbing erection.

Without tearing her glance away from me, she bent forward and reached under the hem of her skirt. For an instant, a fleeting expression of concentration passed across her face. A moment later, she was sliding a wispy pair of black lace panties down over her ankles.

"Come here, Jerry," she said in a hoarse, husky whisper. As she spoke, she lifted the skirt of her flowing dress dramatically, exposing the blond curling hair of her bush. I could see pink lips peeking out at me. I remember being surprised to see that a dean's pussy looked just like anybody else's. I was terrified. But I was so turned on I thought my cock would explode. The combination of fear and sexual excitement was driving me wild.

Perching on the edge of her desk, she raised her skirt around her waist and spread her thighs wantonly. "Come here and fuck me, Jerry," she said. Her voice was firm and controlled.

I hesitated for a moment, knowing that once my cock was inside her there would be no turning back.

Up until now, we had just been fooling around. She would always be able to tell herself that nothing really happened between us. But if I did what she was demanding, there would be no question about it. Getting fucked leaves no doubts.

"Fuck me," she said again.

What could I do? It was a command from the dean. I walked slowly toward her, my cock pointing straight at her open pussy. I was nervous, but I wanted her more than I ever wanted any of the girls I had screwed before. With the young girls, it was fun. But with her, it was urgent business.

The thought of doing it with a woman of her age and experience was super exciting. I guess the best part was that she was the dean and she was spreading her legs for me right there in her office. On the other side of the door, they were running a school. But in here, it was serious sex time. I wanted to say something, but I was afraid of breaking the spell. At last I blurted, "Yes, I want to fuck you."

She groaned and beckoned with her hands. When I stood between her legs, she wrapped them around my waist, drawing me toward her. She leaned back on the desk and closed her eyes as I guided my cock into her opening with my fingers. The thrill as I actually felt it slipping inside her was indescribable. It was like the first time I ever got laid. I just couldn't believe it was actually happening. But the throbbing sensation in my dick was very real.

I wanted to stretch out the penetration so that each second would be a separate experience for me to remember and gloat over later, but her opening just seemed to swallow me up. Her legs tightened around me as she pulled me all the way into her with a single driving thrust. Her pussy gripped my throbbing cock snugly, holding me prisoner in the velvety depths of her body. I froze for a moment, giving her sex muscles a chance to adjust to my thickness. Then I began to move rhythmically in and out.

The movements of our bodies were perfectly synchronized, but I can't take credit for that. Her hips and thighs were choreographing the entire fuck. Her pelvis rocked up and down, controlling the way my cock pleasured her inside. With each rolling motion, her tits bobbed erotically.

I had to struggle to keep from popping my load right then and there. I wanted to be sure that she came before I did. I concentrated on the possibility that we might get caught any minute, hoping that the fear would slow me down. But all it did was get me hotter. I knew I was going to lose it. I didn't know what to do.

Then she started to sob, and I knew that everything was going to be all right. "Oh, you strong young jock," she moaned. "Oh, fuck me hard with your strong young dick. Oh, give it to me. Oh, yes, yes, yes. Fuck me. Fuck me. Fuck me. Oh, God, I'm going to come. Oh, yes, I'm going to come."

At that moment, she stopped being the dean and turned into a sexy she-animal in heat. I knew that she was going to unload her orgasm, and that freed me to let my own come flow. My moans mingled with her cries as I began to pump my spunk into her pussy. Her eyes were tightly shut, and her head was rolling from side to side, telling me that her climax was upon her. I continued driving into her until there was nothing left in me.

By the time my cock softened, it was clear that she was satisfied, too. Her legs relaxed their grip on my waist, and then let go all together. I stepped back. She smiled and stood up, buttoning the front of her dress and slipping back into her panties.

"Thank you, Jerry," she said. "That was wonderful." Then the satisfied smile vanished from her face, and she became businesslike once more. "But I don't think it would be a good idea for us to see each other again."

I realized that I was being put back in my place. I guess I felt better about it that way, too. As I was putting my jock and shorts back on, she said, "I'll talk to Dr. Hoffman. He's chair of the math department. I'm sure that he can help you pass your course."

I never have seen her again, not even walking around the campus. It's just as well, of course. I think about her all the time, though, and about that hot fuck we had on the desk in her office. She was better at sex than any girl I ever had before or since. Maybe it was her experience that made every move seem perfectly planned yet spontaneous at the same time. A lot of it had to do with the situation. Students aren't supposed to fuck the dean, especially in her office, especially on her desk. All of that played a role in making it so different and exciting.

My dad thought that baseball, football, and basketball were the only sports that would pay off. He'll never know how wrong he was. There might not be much money in track, but one thing I know for sure: It was my running that got me the best sex I ever had.

TABOO

Charlotte, forty-six, is recently divorced for the second time. She is five-foot-five, with bright and sparkling blue eyes. In her younger years, she was a high-fashion model whose face graced magazines all over the world. The beauty of her features, the shimmering fire-red tones in her soft brown hair, and the well-tended firmness of her slender body continue to testify to her illustrious career. In recalling the best sex she ever had, Charlotte goes back more than twenty years to a night in Paris.

♥   ♥   ♥

I was born to a wealthy New Orleans family with an old and respected name. Growing up during the forties and fifties, I developed some very strong prejudices. I believed that established families with old money and a heritage that was part of the South's rich history were really the Lord's chosen.

My early education instilled in me the belief that God had created five castes of people. First, there were the privileged class, to which my family belonged. We had been wealthy since the days of slavery, and no one else was our equal. Then there were the nouveau riche with new money that we regarded as less than clean.

Below them were the middle-class people. Almost at the bottom were the working-class people, whom we thought of as white trash. And then there were the blacks. It took me a very long time to grow up and stop thinking like a rich little Southern fool.

Daddy didn't think that a girl of my position should soil herself with a college education, so he sent me to a finishing school. Although it was an all-girls' institution, it was closely associated with a prominent military academy located nearby. I had dozens of young men lining up to beg me for dates. Although I never formed any serious attachments, by the time I was twenty I had slept with several of them. It would be false modesty for me to deny that I was pretty.

Daddy believed that I was pretty enough to be on the cover of a magazine. He always said that a highborn girl shouldn't have a real occupation, but modeling was different. He arranged an interview with an advertising agency owned by one of his friends. They liked me and introduced me to a modeling agent who managed my career. I never got involved in the frenzied rush from one shoot to another like most models do, but I did work on carefully selected assignments.

I was only twenty-two when my agent called to say that I was going to Paris to pose for the cover of a major fashion magazine. I was mildly excited. When he added that the photographer would be Maurice Jourdan, however, I was beside myself. I could have gone to Paris any time I wanted, but the opportunity of being photographed by Maurice Jourdan was unique.

Among the photographic artists of the fashion world, Maurice Jourdan was held in the highest esteem. He was generally recognized as the best in the business. Combined with his rare talent, he had a well-known philosophy.

Jourdan had gone on record as saying that every woman has her own special quality, which he called her "enigmatic essence." A photographer, he said, must first find it. Then he must study it. Then and only then could he hope to capture it on film. A Jourdan shoot took longer than most, because he insisted on spending time getting to know his model before he would consider taking her picture. Everyone agreed that it was worth the extra expense, however, just to have Maurice Jourdan's name associated with the project.

When I arrived at the Paris hotel, there was a sense of commotion in the air and a general feeling of eagerness. The lobby was filled with people waiting to meet the celebrity. My agent advised me to rest in my suite of rooms until the fuss settled down.

When the limo brought Jourdan to the hotel, I wouldn't have been able to get near him anyway. There were paparazzi all over, cameras flashing everywhere. Writers from fashion magazines published all over the world were pushing through the crowds in hopes of getting an interview with this talented artist of the lens.

I waited expectantly in my suite for the message that Mr. Jourdan was ready to meet with me in the hotel restaurant. When my agent escorted me into the room, Maurice stood up to greet me. I was shocked. The last thing in the world I expected to see was a black man. The photographer was tall and very slim, with black eyes and hair. His skin was the color of coal. I did my best to maintain my composure as he pulled a chair out for me.

I was startled when he introduced himself. I never anticipated hearing a black man speak in anything but an uneducated, down-home manner. Jourdan's exquisite French accent made him sound charming and refined. Nevertheless, I felt very uncomfortable, at first, having a conversation with him over a table in a restaurant.

According to everything I was brought up to believe, all black men lived with the dream of some day taking a white woman to bed. Every time he looked at me, I was certain that he was undressing me in his mind. As our conversation progressed, however, I realized that this wasn't so. He was studying me, looking for my enigmatic essence.

When I spoke, he stared deep into my eyes. At one point, he even reached across the table and lightly touched my cheek with his fingertips. I think it was the first time I ever felt a black man's hand on me. By now, I had recovered from my initial discomfort enough to realize that his interest was strictly professional. I forced myself to show my good breeding by not drawing back in horror.

Although our exchange was professional, somewhere inside I realized that there was a streak of sensuality running through it. His voice was soft and seductive, suggestive of clandestine rendezvous in opulent surroundings. In part, his photographic genius came from his genuine love for women.

Every flash of his eyes and every syllable that rolled off his tongue made this clear. Yet there was nothing crude or improper about his manner. He was frank in his appreciation of femininity and completely honest in saying that he found beauty in every woman.

I tried hard to concentrate on the job we were there to do, but I couldn't help daydreaming about sexual intimacies with him. Strange as it was, I found him sexually attractive. Although this was contrary to everything I had been brought up to believe, my upbringing was partially responsible for it.

From the time I was old enough to know the difference between girls and boys, I was taught that it was taboo for white girls to have anything to do with black boys. I was trained to believe that the only thing any black male ever thought about was having sex with a white female. In a hundred different ways, I learned to think of black men as sex-crazed animals, with lust always on their minds.

My training made it impossible for me to sit across a table from this black man without thinking about sex. My head was so awash in erotic imagery that I'm afraid I remember very little of what we talked about. I do recall that as we got up from the table, he said, "You are very beautiful, with a lovely essence. I look forward to working with you. We will start shooting tomorrow morning at nine sharp."

I spent the following day outdoors, posing in front of sights that the world associates with Paris. Working with Maurice was incredible. He knew exactly what he wanted from a model and had a special way of getting it. Before I knew it, the day was over and we were riding together back to the hotel. As I got out of the limo, Maurice said, "I'll let you know when the photos are ready."

That evening I was alone in my suite when the phone rang. It was Maurice saying that the pictures were ready and asking whether he could come and show them to me. A few minutes later he was at my door.

We sat together on the sofa in the sitting room looking at the proofs. They were simply amazing. The face in the pictures was mine, but it managed to convey a personality that seemed foreign to me. The woman standing in front of the Eiffel Tower in a high-fashion gown was the personification of sexuality. Eroticism emanated from every pose. The angle of a shoulder, the tilt of the head, the droop of an eyelid all combined to project a sense of lust and a promise of its fulfillment.

I was so excited by what I saw that almost half an hour passed before I remembered that I was alone in a hotel suite with a black man. By then it was too late. Maurice had conquered me with his vision of my essence. I couldn't help but surrender to him when he stroked my hair for a moment and then embraced me. His lips were soft against mine. His exploring fingers thrilled my hungry body.

Although it violated everything I believed, I knew I wanted him. I wanted to feel him touching me and I wanted to touch him. I wanted to expose my body to the appreciation of his gaze, and I wanted to stare hungrily at his. I sensed his devotion to the erotic and I longed to yield to it. He was a master at lovemaking as he was a master of his art. Every grazing stroke of his fingertips brought me closer to submission.

Through it all, I was acutely aware that he was black. I can't say that it no longer mattered. On the contrary, it seemed to make the entire episode even more exciting. Our contact was forbidden, even though it was exquisite. I felt that I was discovering secrets that no other white woman on the face of the earth had ever discovered before.

In a daze, I let him lead me to the bedroom, where we undressed and fondled each other boldly and freely. Although I had been with other men, no one ever touched me as softly or as sensuously as he did. I had never before reached the heights of pleasure to which he brought me. Every move, every kiss, every stroke was uniquely tailored to my special needs.

When at last he mounted and entered me, I felt my whole body opening to him. As he filled me with the substance of his masculinity, I wrapped myself around him. I was his. For the moment, he was my master. I presented him with my mind and soul as well as my body. My senses submitted to his will, prepared to obey him absolutely. When his movements demanded my orgasm, I gave it to him. We made love until the sun outside our window began lighting the damp Parisian streets.

In the morning over room-service coffee, I asked Maurice to tell me what he had found to be my enigmatic essence. He said it was my unceasing sexuality. He said that sex would always be part of everything I did, part of every gesture I made; that eroticism would accompany the movement of my hand when I stirred sugar into my tea and would drive my car when I stepped on the accelerator.

In the years that followed, I came to fully appreciate how correct Maurice's judgment had been. He saw something in me that I had never seen in myself. He taught me two important lessons that night.

The first was the truth about my sensual nature. By showing it to me, he taught me to see the erotic aspect in every human contact. I learned to banish shame from my existence and to dedicate myself to the fulfillment of my sexual destiny.

The second lesson was that the real differences in men do not lie in their skin color. I have been married twice and have had many lovers. Maurice was the most perfect sex mate I have ever known. The reason wasn't just physical. Although he was black, his body was like any other man's. His penis wasn't bigger or harder or thicker, as I always imagined a black man's would be. His lust wasn't bestial or base, as I had been taught to expect.

What made Maurice special was his passion for sex and his genuine love and respect for all women. This made the photos that he took of me the best I've ever seen. And it made our sex the best I ever had.

2

A DREAM COME TRUE

Many people become grouchy if they don't get enough sleep. Recent experiments indicate, however, that it might not be sleep deprivation that makes a person tense the next morning. The real root of the problem may lie in an insufficient opportunity to dream.

In these experiments, two groups slept under controlled conditions every night for a period of several weeks. The members of one group were interrupted whenever their rapid eye movements, or REMs, indicated that they were beginning to dream. Members of the other group were woken up as often, but only when they were not dreaming. As a result, the two groups got approximately the same amount of sleep, but one was permitted to dream and the other was not.

Those allowed to dream experienced no significant change in attitude or behavior. In a relatively short time, however, those who had been prevented from dreaming began to show signs of tension and irritability. Some developed symptoms of severe mental illness and had to be eliminated from the program. These people recovered shortly after returning to their normal dream patterns.

The obvious conclusion is that we need to dream.

Dreams allow our unconscious minds to give expression to secrets that we hide even from ourselves. When these secrets are happy ones, our dreams are pleasant. When the secrets are not happy ones, we have nightmares.

The dreams we have while awake are called *daydreams* or *fantasies*. Unlike those that come to us in our sleep, they are usually subject to our conscious control. This is why we do not have "daymares."

Daydreams are also important. They provide us with escape from a reality that, at times, can seem overpoweringly oppressive. They allow us to be what otherwise we might not ever be able to be. They allow us to do what, otherwise, we might not ever be able to do. In daydreams we can fulfill our most impossible wishes.

The things we wish for and daydream about are not always impossible, though. Sometimes life surprises us with experiences that we imagined but never really believed could happen. When this occurs, we have the sense of a dream coming true. The people whose stories are told in this chapter had sexual contacts that they had fantasized about without ever expecting to experience. The unanticipated fulfillment of their secret wishes led them to regard their dreams-come-true as the best sex they ever had.

EQUESTRIAN FANTASY

Barrie is forty-two years old. Her five-foot-seven-inch frame carries a voluptuous fleshiness that brings to mind a painting by Rubens. She wears her wavy chestnut hair long and loose. The color of her eyes, just a shade darker than her hair, emphasizes the olive of her complexion. Barrie's husband, Gordon, owns a car dealership, which he inherited from his father. Barrie says that the best sex she ever had was on the day Gordon became the handsome prince of her adolescent dreams.

♥ ♥ ♥

About four years ago, Gordon and I found the vacation home that we had been searching for. It's an old stone house in the woods on three hundred acres of land in the heart of Washington's timber country. It's only a few hours' drive from the city where we live, but it feels like another world. As soon as we saw it, we knew it was for us. I liked the seclusion, but I think that what appealed most to Gordon was that the place needed a lot of fixing up. He said that working with his hands on the weekend would help him relax after a hard week in the city.

Cedar and pine and fir trees grow over most of the land, but the area around the house is clear. There are a few outbuildings, a small barn, and a corral. When we bought the place, there was a white horse in our corral. It belonged to Fred Conklin, a neighbor who was in the process of building a new barn on his own land. When we moved in, Fred offered to remove the horse to a temporary shed that he had constructed, but I told him it wouldn't be necessary. I liked seeing the horse there.

Fred told me that he didn't have time to do much riding and that we could ride Gunner whenever we wanted to. He said that Gunner was an old reliable trail horse who had been ridden through these woods for more than twenty years and probably knew them better than any human ever could. He frequently let Gunner out in the morning to graze on whatever wild grasses he could find. In the evening, Gunner always returned to the corral, where his oats and hay were waiting.

Fred said that if Gordon and I really wanted to become familiar with our property, we ought to climb onto Gunner's back and let him go wherever he wanted. Sooner or later we'd get to see all of our land that way. Fred said that Gunner was strong enough to carry two people. I liked the idea at once.

I had done quite a bit of riding when I was a girl. In fact, I had my first sexual experience while riding a horse. I'll never forget the first time that it happened to me. My parents had given me a chestnut quarter horse for my fourteenth birthday. I used to ride every day after school.

At first I was real nervous. I'd cling to the pommel of my saddle so hard that my knuckles would turn white. After a while, though, I became more confident. Soon I was even riding without a saddle. That's how it happened.

I would bridle the horse and throw a thin blanket over his back. Then I would ride the neighborhood trails, holding on with my legs. As I bounced up and down against the horse's backbone, I would get a warm sensation between my thighs. I didn't quite know what it was, but I knew that it felt good. Sometimes, when I was sitting in my class at school, I would daydream about riding. But I'm sure it was really that tingly feeling that I would be thinking about.

Then one day it happened. I was deliberately bouncing and rubbing myself against the horse's back, feeling the sensation getting more and more intense. The crotch of my panties was getting moist, and I knew somehow that it wasn't the horse's sweat that was making me wet. Suddenly, with a gush of excitement, I exploded.

For what seemed like an eternity, the rest of the world disappeared. I felt like I was spinning in the vortex of a giant whirlpool. It was a little frightening, because I felt that I had totally lost control of myself and my emotions. But it was wonderful. I hoped that it would never end and for a while I thought it wouldn't. When it was over, I struggled to catch my breath, suddenly realizing that I was still on horseback and that not very much time had passed at all. I rode home immediately.

The next day, I hurried to go riding after school again. This time I knew that I was riding for that feeling. I positioned myself as far forward as possible so that my pelvis was pressed tight against the base of the horse's neck. With every step, the movements of his head rubbed his rigid backbone against the sensitive tissues between my legs. I hadn't ridden half a mile when I felt the explosion begin. This time when it was over, I kept riding until I made it happen again.

After that, I realized that I was in control. I could bring on that wonderful feeling any time I wanted to. A few months later one of the girls at school mentioned the word *orgasm,* and all the other girls said that they hoped they would get to have one some day. It was then that I realized what had been happening to me every afternoon when I rode my horse. I never told the other girls, though. It was my little secret.

I began experimenting with different gaits and speeds, seating myself in various positions until I became an expert at masturbating on horseback. Eventually, I discovered that I could bring on the orgasms more quickly and make them more intense if I didn't wear underwear. I would ride in a long flared skirt, spreading it out around me so that no one would know that I was naked underneath it or that I was rubbing myself against the horse through the thin saddle blanket.

As my orgasms approached, I found myself fantasizing about a tall handsome Prince Charming who had scooped me up and carried me off on the back of his glistening white horse. He would make passionate love to me while his horse bounded over hills and dales on the way to his castle. Somehow we were always naked in my fantasy, except for the gold crown which he wore on his head and that never seemed to bounce off.

These were the thoughts that were going through my mind the first time I rode Gunner. Fred Conklin had an old saddle, but he said that Gunner was used to being ridden bareback. When he offered me a saddle blanket and suggested that I just throw it over Gunner's back and climb on, I couldn't help smiling to myself.

I hadn't ridden since my teens, and it never occurred to me that I would experience those wonderful erotic sensations on horseback again now that I was an adult. But I did. I was wearing an old pair of faded Levi's that I'd had for so long that they were perfectly molded to my body. When I threw my leg over Gunner's back, the fabric pulled tight against my crotch, exciting me in a strange but familiar way and making me feel warm all over. I realized at once that it wasn't the jeans that were turning me on so much as it was my recollection of those adolescent experiences.

It took a moment for me to settle comfortably on the horse and I wiggled about, seeking the right position. As I did so, I could feel Gunner's back caressing my sex through my jeans. I became moist almost at once.

I took Fred's advice, letting Gunner walk wherever he pleased. After a few minutes, I began moving my body in rhythm with his steps, remembering things about riding that I had thought I had forgotten. Soon it felt natural to just flow along with the animal. I didn't even have to think about what I was doing.

As the forest swallowed us, I gazed around at the scenery, unconsciously enjoying the warm sensation in that secret spot between my legs. It was like having my adolescent experiences all over again. Only it was better now. When I was a teenager, every sexual sensation was new to me, and sometimes the newness distracted me from the pleasure. But now I was an adult. I knew all about sex. None of the sensations was new. There was no confusion, no uncertainty. There was nothing but pleasure. I was free to enjoy it in a way I never could have as an innocent young girl.

I could feel my nipples hardening against the inside of my bra. I suppose the same thing must have happened when I was fourteen, but I can't remember being aware of it then. I pressed the palms of my hands against my breasts, feeling them tingle at my own touch. The heat of sexual passion was rising quickly inside me.

Gripping Gunner tightly with my legs, I began rocking my groin against his back. Each movement made me wetter. Every step that he took bounced me against him and made my tissues throb with pleasure. As I felt a climax overtaking me, I shut my eyes tightly, returning to my teenage world of discovery. When the first wave of ecstasy washed over me, I had a fleeting image of a naked Prince Charming in a gold crown penetrating me with his massive penis.

After that, I took Gunner out almost every weekend, usually while Gordon was fixing or building something in the house. Gunner was an easy horse to ride, and I had a feeling of total confidence as he walked or loped through the forest. I enjoyed exploring the woods at the whim of the horse. Most of all, I enjoyed the secret orgasms that I had on Gunner's back. Each time I came, I relived the fantasy of sex on horseback. It was still a handsome prince who made love to me while carrying me off to his castle. But now the prince had Gordon's face.

After my rides, I would tell Gordon about the beautiful places I had seen. But I didn't tell him about the orgasms. I guess I was a little embarrassed. After all, I wasn't a kid anymore; I was a married woman. I was afraid that Gordon would wonder why I didn't just ride back and make love to him when I was feeling sexy. I was afraid that he'd get jealous of my riding.

One day, Gunner took me to a spot I had never seen before. It was located deep in the forest, where the trees were so thick that the sun couldn't shine through. Suddenly, Gunner stepped into a clearing where the light was dazzling. It felt like we had entered another world. I could feel the sun's heat beating down against me in sharp contrast to the cool damp of the forest. There was a little pond, and the air was absolutely still except for the sound of unseen birds in the treetops. It was the most picturesque place on our property.

I couldn't wait for Gordon to see it. On the ride back, I paid careful attention to its location so that I could be sure of finding it again. When I described it to Gordon, he was intrigued. He agreed to visit the spot with me the following weekend.

Some time during that week, I decided to try and live out my adolescent dream with Gordon. In preparation for the weekend, I went to a Western-wear shop in the city and bought a long, flared skirt with fringe around the hem. It reminded me of the skirt I wore to ride in when I was young. I know it sounds funny, but I found myself becoming sexually aroused just trying it on. I also bought a loose-fitting white blouse with a scoop neckline and little rhinestones sewn onto it.

I was nervous all week, obsessed with the idea of making my dream come true. I could think of nothing else. It seemed as though the weekend would never arrive.

Saturday morning, as we drove to the woods, Gordon chatted gaily about all the work he was going to accomplish on the house. But I had other ideas. As soon as we arrived, I ran into the bedroom and changed into my cowgirl blouse and skirt. I wore no bra or panties.

When Gordon saw me in my new outfit, he grinned. He said he loved the way the blouse and skirt looked on me. But of course, he had no idea of what it meant to me.

"Come on," I said. "Let's go riding. It's a perfect day to see that pond I told you about, Gordon."

Before he had a chance to answer, I grabbed his hand and led him out to the corral. When Gunner saw us coming, he whinnied and walked toward the gate. He stood patiently while I fitted him with the bridle and threw the blanket over him.

Gordon put one foot on a fence rail and lifted himself athletically onto Gunner's back. Then, reaching down like the prince of my dreams, he lifted me up to sit in front of him. The horse rode off confidently, accepting both of us with ease.

I took the reins as Gordon placed his hands on my waist. Although Gunner was accustomed to select his own trails, he responded willingly to the signals that I gave him. I headed him toward the pond, leaning back against the strength of Gordon's chest. "Hold me tighter," I said. "It feels so good."

Gordon put his arms around me, caressing my belly with his fingertips. I could feel his hands stealing up to stroke the undercurves of my breasts. When he realized that I was not wearing a bra, he drew his breath in. "Naughty little cowgirl," he said. "I wonder what you have in mind."

I giggled like a schoolgirl and shimmied from side to side, rubbing my back against him. "Isn't this fun?" I whispered. "Just the two of us riding together around our property."

Gordon responded by kissing me lightly behind my ear. The touch of his lips filled my loins with desire. The day, the horse, the scenery, the ride, all came together so very perfectly. My excitement was building as I thought about the dream that I had nurtured since my teens and that I hoped was now about to be realized.

The forest was becoming denser, the shade deepening as the sun fought vainly to penetrate the thick canopy of leaves above us. Then, as the darkness was about to become overwhelming, Gunner stepped into the clearing. For a moment we were blinded by the sudden reflection of the sun on the smooth surface of the pond.

"Wow," Gordon gasped. "Barrie, I think we've just entered Shangri-La." I could feel his excitement. "I never imagined anything so beautiful," he said. "And it all belongs to us." He swung down from Gunner's back and reached up for my hand. We walked to the edge of the pond and stood staring at it together in silence.

"Someday we should have a picnic here," I said. Then, taking his hand, I added, "But now let's get back on Gunner. I want to show you something else."

Gordon climbed up onto the horse's back and reached out to help me up. But, stepping on a tree stump, I straddled Gunner with my back to the horse's neck and faced Gordon.

My husband laughed. "Hey," he said. "Thinking of joining the circus? You're sitting backward."

"Not a circus," I said. "But the show is just beginning." With that, I crossed my arms in front of me and took the hem of my blouse in both hands. I gazed into Gordon's eyes for a moment, and then stripped the blouse off over my head with a single swift movement.

The cool air of the forest felt good against my bare breasts, and I felt my nipples harden immediately. Gordon sighed before burying his face in the valley of my cleavage. I tangled my fingers in his hair and moved his head so that his lips were against one of my swollen nipples. I felt him suck hungrily at it, his tongue stroking gently at the sensitive flesh.

I moaned as Gunner took a tentative step forward. The rippling muscles in his back caressed my bare vagina through the thin fabric of the saddle blanket. Gordon continued licking my breasts, unaware that I was naked under my skirt. As Gunner began walking out of the clearing, Gordon leaned back to watch my breasts bounce with each of the horse's movements.

It was exciting to see my husband stare at me that way. Languidly, I leaned back against the horse's neck, gazing at the bulge that Gordon's erection made in the front of his pants. He saw where I was looking and grinned. "Do you think we can do it on horseback?" he asked.

I just smiled and lifted my skirt slowly, exposing my knees and thighs to his lustful gaze. As I raised the garment higher, I saw his penis twitch against the fabric of his trousers. Then, at once, I pulled the skirt all the way up, showing him my nakedness.

Reaching forward, I undid his zipper and freed his huge erection from the confinement of his pants. There was a drop of moisture at its tip. "Yes, Gordon," I said. "I think we can do it on horseback."

Gunner seemed to sense our need and stopped, waiting for his next command. I slithered toward my husband, wrapping my legs around his waist to draw my sex closer to his rigid penis. Lifting myself onto his lap, I moved my hips from side to side until my moist opening found the tip of his manhood. I felt him rock slowly, easing himself forward until he was barely inside me. A groan tore involuntarily from my throat.

I closed my eyes and imagined that I was a teenage girl in the arms of a charming prince. The fantasy was complete. We were astride his noble charger in the woods that surrounded his castle. His strong hands were upon my shoulders, drawing me closer as his probing member gently plunged my dewy depths. I wanted to swallow his hardness into my tunnel, but I remained passive, submitting to his strength and nobility.

I had found the prince of my adolescent fantasies. He was about to take me, to make me his completely. As our bodies joined, I could almost see the golden crown upon his head. I never felt so fulfilled, so wanton, so complete. It was as though I had been waiting for this moment ever since that first explosion in my teen years. It was as though all of life had been nothing more than a background for my dream of love on the back of a horse.

Inside me, there was a climax building of such intensity that at first it baffled and confused me. It was like nothing I had ever felt before. It was new. It was incredible. It was perfect. It was there. When it hit, I rocked forward furiously, aware that Gordon was exploding at precisely the same moment.

All time stopped. The universe was ours alone. We filled it with our ecstasy, moaning and sobbing the sounds of our pleasure to a silent, secret forest. It was perfect. It was more than I ever could have imagined.

A century later, we became aware again of our surroundings, even more beautiful now that they had been the backdrop for our shared love. Gunner was in motion, heading back to the house without any further instruction from me. He seemed to know that our visit to the forest was complete, that there was nothing more that we could take from nature that day.

Since then, Gordon and I have made love in the forest many times. Occasionally, we bring a blanket to our little pond and make passionate love in the dazzling light of the clearing. We both feel that we have achieved erotic perfection. But I'll never forget that wonderful day when my Prince Charming made love to me on his handsome steed. No matter what else I ever experience, I will always think of that day as the best sex I ever had.

APRIL'S SECRET DREAM

April *is thirty-four and recently divorced. At five-foot-six, she is slim with a boyish figure that allows her to go braless most of the time. Her short brown hair frames a gamine face with brown saucer eyes that wear an expression of perpetual curiosity. April works as a secretary in the office of a large insurance company. She is a little nervous as she tells us about an experience that she frequently imagined but never expected to have.*

♥　　♥　　♥

My marriage to Bill was a total disaster right from the very beginning. I guess our personalities just weren't compatible. We fought over everything, rarely had fun together, and worst of all, didn't even have good sex. For some reason which I still don't understand, I stuck it out for nine years. Then everything fell apart. The only way for either of us to keep our sanity was to get divorced. I think our divorce was the only thing we didn't argue about.

Bill is a fairly successful architect, and I never had to work during our marriage. Even after the divorce, he agreed to a substantial settlement so that I still wouldn't have to work if I didn't want to. But the first thing I did was take word-processing courses so I could go out and get a job. Otherwise, I think I would have gone crazy. I needed to meet people and I couldn't think of any other way.

The insurance company I work for owns and occupies an entire seven-story building. We even have our own cafeteria and health club. I've made quite a few friends there. Unfortunately, they're all women. It's amazing how many women my age are divorced or separated and in the same situation as I.

We talk to each other about our problems all the time, but that doesn't solve them. Before my divorce, Bill and I hardly ever had sex. Afterward, it didn't get any better. If I didn't do myself, I wouldn't get any at all.

I never masturbated much, even when I was a kid. I had a fairly strict religious upbringing. Deep down, I always believed that sex wasn't really permissible unless it was aimed at reproduction. After the divorce, though, there were times when my urges would overcome me, and I would rub myself with my fingers until I found relief. I got the idea to buy a vibrator after listening to one of the women at the office describe the pleasure that it gave her to use one.

It's amazing how very explicit the conversations would get around lunch tables in the office cafeteria. Some of the women described their sex experiences in such intimate detail that I would feel a burning itch in my loins for the rest of the afternoon. Then in the evening I would spend hours alone in bed playing with my vibrator and imagining the acts and intimacies that they had discussed.

Once, one of the women told about a time that Pat, a female claims adjuster, made a pass at her. She turned Pat down, of course. Then she took advantage of the first available opportunity to talk about it at lunch. I was shocked to learn that Pat was a lesbian. She was pretty and feminine-looking, with blond hair, a knock-out figure, and the kind of big breasts that men die for. I just couldn't believe that anyone who looked like Pat would be interested in having sex with another woman. I wondered what sorts of things two women would do.

Later that night, when I was in bed touching myself, I pictured Pat touching another woman that way. I was horrified by the idea, but a little fascinated by it, too, I guess. As I imagined two women fingering each other and caressing each other's breasts, I came to a fast and powerful orgasm. After that, I frequently conjured up the same image deliberately to excite myself when masturbating.

I never would have admitted that to anyone, because it seemed so unnatural and sinful. Yet I couldn't think of a sexier fantasy. When I fantasized about men, it sometimes took me a long, long time to have a climax. But picturing two women together never failed to bring me to a swift and satisfying finish.

That's probably why I was so nervous when Pat stepped up to my table one afternoon while I was having lunch alone. "Do you mind if I join you?" she asked.

If I could have thought of a believable excuse, I would have. But there just wasn't any graceful way out. "Not at all," I said hesitantly. "I'm almost through anyway."

The big-bosomed claims adjuster set her tray on the table and sat in the chair opposite mine. "I'm Pat," she said with a friendly smile. "I work on the fifth floor." She was so warm that I was immediately at ease.

"I know," I said. "I've seen you around." Remembering my manners, I added, "I'm April."

"As fresh as a spring shower," Pat quipped.

54

THE BEST SEX I EVER HAD

I found myself liking this friendly woman. Conversation flowed so easily between us that for a while I forgot she was gay. She was just like anyone else, and nicer than lots of people I've known. We chatted about the weather and about events in the office, and discussed all the things that people talk about when they are getting acquainted. By the time lunch was over, we had become friends.

It wasn't until later that night that I remembered Pat's sexual preference. I was watching television when my mind started wandering. I found myself trying to imagine what she'd look like without her clothes on and what she would do with another woman. The thoughts aroused me so much that I felt all moist and tingly.

Without even bothering to turn off the TV, I reached for my vibrator, slipped out of my jeans and panties, and began pleasuring myself. I closed my eyes and pictured Pat's huge breasts, imagining that her pink nipples were erect. My orgasm came almost immediately, rolling over me like a tidal wave. When it was through, I realized to my shock that my last mental image as I skyrocketed to ecstasy was of Pat's naked body.

Later, as I lay in bed, I pondered the strange thoughts that I was having. I couldn't understand why I pictured a nude woman while masturbating or why my mind kept turning to fantasies of two women together. I knew that I found the idea fascinating and extremely exciting, and this scared me.

It was against everything I believed in. When I was young I was taught that sex was for making babies. I know that most of the time it doesn't lead to that, but at least between a man and woman it's always a possibility. Between two women, there can never be anything more than lust. Maybe that's what intrigued me so much about it.

I lay awake most of the night, feeling guilty about my fantasies. Then, toward morning, I began to see it in a different light. Fantasies are like dreams. There's nothing wrong with dreaming. If the thought of sex between women was exciting to me, I was entitled to amuse myself with it. As long as it was only a thought, how could it hurt? I made up my mind to put guilt aside. My dreams were harmless, and there was no reason why I shouldn't have them.

Pat and I had lunch together frequently after that. I looked forward to my conversations with her. They were personal and candid, but the topic of sex was never a part of them. She did mention once that she was homosexual, but neither of us brought it up again. We started seeing each other outside the office, meeting occasionally for dinner or a drink. I began to think of Pat as one of my closest friends.

Sometimes in the evening when I was alone at home playing with myself, I allowed myself to imagine Pat doing things to me. I pictured her hands and even her lips bringing pleasure to the sensitive tissues of my body. I tried to move my fingers as I thought she would do. When I stroked my pleasure button with the tip of my vibrator, I pretended Pat was holding it. There were times I felt guilty, but I reminded myself that it was only a dream and that it could never actually happen in real life.

During the day, when I was having lunch with Pat and chatting about everyday activities, I wondered what Pat would think if she knew the role she played in my dreams. I also wondered if she ever fantasized about having sex with me. I toyed with the idea of asking her, but then decided it was best if I kept my secret dreams to myself. I was afraid that bringing sex out into the open would somehow spoil our friendship.

By this time, our relationship had come to mean a great deal to me. That's why I was so upset when Pat broke the news. She told me she had been offered a great job in another city and that she had accepted it. She would be moving away in just a few weeks. I was devastated.

In the time that remained, Pat and I saw more of each other than ever before. I helped get her things together for the move, filling out dozens of change-of-address cards and hauling empty cartons from the grocery store for packing. I knew that I was going to miss my new friend terribly.

On her last day at the office, there was a little party for her. Drinks were served, and by the time it was over, I was already feeling a little tipsy. After work, I went with Pat to her apartment to help with last-minute details. When we finished putting the last strip of tape on the last of the cartons, Pat took a bottle of wine from the cabinet.

"I saved the good stuff for a going-away celebration," she said, removing the cork and tipping the bottle into a couple of glasses.

Raising mine, I toasted, "To your continued success and our continued friendship." Pat hugged me warmly before we sipped together.

We drained the bottle completely and were into a second one before I realized it. "I'm really going to miss you, Pat," I said, copious tears flowing down my cheeks. "You're the best friend I've had." My shoulders started to shake as I began sobbing.

Pat moved over next to me on the couch and placed a comforting arm around me. "We'll still be in touch, April," she said. "We can talk on the phone every day."

Her tenderness touched me so that I started crying even harder. Pat held me tighter, stroking my hair and murmuring words of comfort. When I buried my face in her shoulder, sobbing like a child, she kissed my forehead lightly. "Don't cry, April," she whispered.

The next thing I knew, she was kissing me on the lips. It was a soft and friendly kiss at first. Without thinking, I returned it. It felt like a natural exchange between close friends. Gradually, her lips increased the pressure, and so did mine. Before either of us realized what was happening, the contact became passionate.

I felt her nibbling at my lips, alternately tantalizing them with soft strokes of her tongue and pressing them heatedly. Involuntarily, I responded, kissing her as I had never kissed Bill. Our tongues played hide-and-seek from her mouth to mine. Our breathing became deep and labored. The tension that I was feeling began to dissolve, leaving me comfortable and relaxed in the arms of my woman friend.

Once it began, our embrace moved forward without shame or hesitation. Pat cradled me in the encircling security of her arms. Her hands moved over my back, petting and stroking me until I felt like purring. She pressed the front of her body against mine, exciting me with the softness of her breasts. "I want to touch you," she whispered, slipping one of her hands under my sweater. I was wearing no bra.

I trembled, not with fear but with burning excitement, as her gentle fingers moved over the smooth skin of my belly, exploring higher until they found the small mounds of my breasts. At first she stroked little circles around their quivering tips, as if afraid that direct contact would break the spell. My nipples were hard, and I wanted her to touch them. I moved my body to bring her fingertips into contact with the turgid buttons.

When I first felt her fingers grazing them, I moaned softly with pleasure. Emboldened by the sound, Pat took the erect cones between her thumbs and fore-fingers, rolling them expertly until my entire body was on fire. I had fantasized about her doing this to me so many times that her touch felt almost familiar. I closed my eyes and allowed the waves of pleasure to engulf me.

I wanted to touch her, too. More than anything, I wanted to see her breasts. I didn't know what to say. I didn't know what to do. Reading my mind, Pat leaned away from me and unbuttoned her blouse. I became frantically excited at the glimpse of white lace that covered her. Without a thought, I reached out, placing my hands inside her open blouse and running my fingers over the delicate fabric of her undergarment.

"Oh," I said. "You have such big, beautiful breasts."

"Would you like to see them?" Pat asked softly in a trembling voice. I realized that she was even more nervous than I was.

"Ooh, yes," I answered, reaching behind her to undo hooks and eyes with shaking fingers. Gracefully, she moved her arms and slipped out of blouse and bra in one quick gesture. Her breasts were high and round, with nipples even bigger and pinker than I had imagined. I was in awe. "Pat," I whispered. "I always wished I had boobs like yours. They're beautiful."

Pat cupped the two globes in her hands and held them up to me. "I've been dying to show them to you," she said. "And I've been dying to see yours."

Without waiting for further encouragement, I stripped my sweater over my head. I had always felt that my breasts were too small and unfemi-nine, but the excited gasp that came from Pat's lips made me feel good about them. "I love your little titties," my friend whispered, moving her hands from her own large breasts to my small ones. My nipples were so hard that they felt like rocks. I closed my eyes and let her thrill me.

"I want to see all of you," Pat said eagerly. "Let's both get completely naked."

I don't remember either of us undressing, but within moments our clothes were scattered carelessly around the room, and we were looking hungrily at each other's bodies. Pat groaned when she saw my thick and tangled bush. Hers was sparser, the curling golden hair looking soft and silky.

"I want to touch your breasts," I murmured, nervous with excitement. Without waiting another moment, I took the ripe mounds in my hands. I had never touched another woman's boobs before. I couldn't believe how good it felt.

When my hands started to knead and squeeze the resilient flesh, her nipples swelled up like cherries. Instinctively, I took one in my mouth, sucking lightly on it. Then I held both of them in my hands. Pat's moan of pleasure excited me. It was thrilling to give so much satisfaction to another person.

I was getting to live out the dream that I had been enjoying for so many lonely nights. As in the fantasy, I felt Pat's hands on my small breasts, twirling the erect nipples. I tried to follow her example, attempting to touch her in exactly the same way she was touching me.

We sat naked on the couch for a long time, each of us holding the other's breasts, each of us demonstrating to the other what pleased us most. When her fingers found an especially sensitive place on my nipples, I looked for the corresponding spot on hers.

We learned about ourselves and each other as we enjoyed our mutual exploration.

I sucked on Pat's cherry nipples, rolling my tongue over their erectness while listening to my friend's sensuous moans. Leaning back, I closed my eyes to let her suck on mine. Her tongue traced circles around them, bringing me more pleasure than I had ever known.

I was so wet between the legs that I could feel moisture coating the white skin of my inner thighs. In my dreams, Pat always did mysterious things to me down there. I wondered if anything like that could really happen. The more I thought about it, the more I wanted it.

While Pat's lips were nibbling at the ends of my breasts, I boldly placed my hand on the back of her head. Pressing gently, I guided her face downward until her mouth moved lower and lower across my belly. At last I could feel her hot breath against the lips of my opening. For a moment, I was scared. Excitement replaced fear when I felt her kissing lightly at my feminine tissues.

Nothing in my life ever felt that good. Bill never put his mouth anywhere near my sex. The closest I ever came to experiencing it before was in my dreams. And then it was always Pat who was doing it. Now, as her mouth glided over my vulva, my hot passion mingled with the excitement of living out a fantasy that I had never expected to come true.

Even in my dreams, I didn't imagine specifically what her mouth would be doing to me. Every touch of her lips and tongue was an exciting surprise. I felt her nibble at my sensitive membranes, the grazing softness of her lips opening me farther and farther. Then I felt the tip of her tongue sink inside with a gentleness that a penis could never master. It drove deeper and deeper until I could feel the lips of her mouth press against my sex lips.

I groaned, my eyes shut tightly. Fantastic images were spinning in my brain while thrills of erotic excitement set me quivering. I could almost see the droplets of moisture that oozed from me. I could almost taste the spice of the lovejuices that flowed so freely.

I wanted to do to Pat the things she was doing to me. I wanted to see her opening, to smell it, to press my face into it. I wanted to tongue her the same way she was tonguing me. I wanted to give back some of the pleasure I was receiving.

Pat must have sensed my hunger. Guiding me with hands on my naked hips, she moved me from the couch to the carpeted floor. I lay on my back with my legs splayed wide, my womanhood completely open to her gaze, to her touch, vulnerable to anything she wanted to do to it. Pat straddled me, her knees on either side of my head, her body facing my feet. The open gash of her turgid vagina was just above my mouth.

I had never really seen a woman's sex organ up close before. Not even my own. Pat's was beautiful. It looked like an exotic flower, a lovely rose-colored orchid. She lowered her face until her lips and tongue were in contact again with my female opening. This brought her crotch lower until it was floating just above me.

I inhaled, smelling the fragrant musk of her excited femininity. I wanted to taste her. Raising my head slightly, I pressed my lips against the glistening membranes. In my dreams, I had always been the recipient of pleasure. I had never even imagined doing what I was doing now. My excitement overcame me, though, and I reached tentatively out with my tongue to lap fascinatedly at Pat's labia. I couldn't believe how exotically good she tasted.

Becoming bolder, I began to lick her crack with the same enthusiasm that she showed as she licked me. Simultaneously, we plunged each other's depths with swabbing strokes of our tongues. I felt her mouth working its way higher, toward the quivering point of desire at the head of my clitoris. When she dabbed it carefully with the tip of her tongue, the sensation was exquisite. An involuntary cry of excitement tore from my throat. Encouraged by it, Pat began sucking my little love button hungrily, making me sob and pant with delight.

Wanting to give her as much pleasure as she was giving me, I began searching for the center of her sex, moving my tongue in widening circles until it encountered the erection of her clit. Her hips bucked wildly, pressing her dampness against my face. I continued to explore her lingually, searching for the most sensitive spot.

Pat groaned loudly in response to my gentle sucking of her clitoris. The sound made her lips and throat vibrate, tantalizing my ganglion until I thought I would die of pleasure. She lapped figure eights around my button, setting off a series of bubbling reactions in my loins. I reciprocated, sucking her sex as though I had been doing it all my life.

When I felt her jerk, I knew instinctively that her climax was beginning. My own was forming too, like a volcano beneath the surface of my sex. It was burgeoning, looming larger and higher with each breath I took. I wanted to postpone it for as long as I could, to put it off so that I could concentrate all my energies on my friend and on her sexual satisfaction.

I opened my eyes to stare at the drooling opening of her sex, my mouth working her clit feverishly. I was sure that I could taste the juices of her orgasm flowing. Her body was twitching and convulsing uncontrollably, waves of pleasure robbing her of all control. When she reached the peak of ecstasy, she screamed once, long and loud.

I knew that was the signal for me to let myself go. Groaning and sobbing, I poured forth the pent-up energy of sexual release. Flashes of pleasure wracked my body, making me roll and writhe beneath her. All the while, her lips continued nibbling at me, bringing shuddering wave after shuddering wave to my exploding groin. I had never dreamed anything could feel this good. It was the longest and the best orgasm I ever had in my life.

We seemed to drift into a state of semiconsciousness for a while. When I was aware again of what was happening, I found us lying side by side exhausted on the floor. Pat was worried, apparently concerned that this unexpected experience would damage our friendship. "April," she said. "I didn't mean for this ..."

I just giggled. "It was the best sex I ever had," I said, putting her at ease. "It was a wonderful going-away present we gave to each other. I'll remember it for the rest of my life."

I've never had another experience with Pat, or with any other woman, for that matter. I guess it was just a one-time thing. But I'm not the least bit sorry about it. Sometimes it seems like just another one of those sexy masturbation fantasies that I dream when I play with myself at night. It really happened, though. I'm glad my dream came true.

3

SPONTANEOUS COMBUSTION

A marriage counselor once told a couple that their relationship would improve if they injected more spontaneity into their sex life. "Instead of planning it, just make love whenever the mood strikes," she advised them. On their next visit to her office, the couple reported that they had taken her advice and that, although their marriage had improved as a result, they were no longer welcome in their favorite restaurant.

Sexual urges are not the products of discipline or training. They are always bubbling in the caldera of our unconscious minds. Like lava, they spring forth whenever they find an opening, regardless of any sense of propriety about time or place.

Predetermining when and where sexual intercourse will occur is like attempting to tame the forces of Nature itself. The results are often disastrous. Sex loses its novelty when it becomes scheduled or routine. This may cause a relationship to grow stale and lackluster. The excitement of making love on impulse can restore the glitter, even if it does offend the headwaiter.

There is, of course, a middle ground. Life offers many opportunities for indulging erotic desires without falling to the floor in the local supermarket or coupling on the photocopy machine in the middle of the office. Adventurous couples can always find a place for unscheduled sex without risking arrest for public lewdness.

The people who tell their stories in this chapter are of different ages and varied walks of life. What they have in common is that they all discovered the benefits of sexual spontaneity. The joy that is apparent as they recount their experiences is a suggestion of the pleasures that await those who are willing to change their plans at a moment's notice to accommodate their sexual needs.

A WALK IN THE WOODS

Donna is in her late fifties and does not attempt to hide it. She wears no makeup. Her gray hair is cut short and brushed back in a simple, natural style. Her flashing blue eyes and even white teeth give her a healthy appearance. She is about five-foot-two and slight. Her skin is taut and smooth. She attributes her youthfulness to proper diet. Her husband, Hal, sixty-one, is a retired postal worker. Donna smiles as she remembers an afternoon about a year ago when she and Hal experienced their best sex.

♥   ♥   ♥

Everybody seems to be obsessed with physical fitness these days, but Hal and I have never really gotten in to it. The closest we come to being athletic is when we take our walks. When the weather is nice, we try to get out two or three times a week. Sometimes it takes quite some doing, because deep down we're both terribly lazy.

Usually, if we find a scenic place for a walk, we go back again. It's kind of an incentive to get us up and off our asses. Once we discovered a beautiful trail up by the lake. From the parking lot, through the woods, to the edge of the lake and back came to about two miles. Just right for a couple of couch potatoes like us.

The first time we went there, we were surprised that we had the whole place to ourselves. The walk took a little less than an hour, and we didn't see another soul in all that time. That certainly appealed to us. It was so nice and peaceful. When we got back to the car, we decided that we'd walk there again the next day. That was a Saturday, and we did see a few people, but it was still pretty secluded.

The third time we went there, it was a weekday and we were sure we'd be alone. The sun was hot, and after we had walked for ten minutes or so, Hal decided to take off his shirt and tie it around his waist. After that, he couldn't seem to stop talking about how good the sun felt on his bare skin. It was making me jealous.

"That's not fair," I said. "If you get to go without a shirt, I should, too." I don't think I was really serious, but Hal jumped at the idea.

"Go ahead," he said. "Take it off. I'd like to be able to watch your boobs bounce. It would make the walk a lot more interesting."

Maybe I thought he was kidding; I don't know. I do know that as I started undoing the buttons of my shirt, I was expecting him to stop me. But he didn't. I wondered what he would do if I took off my bra, too. It was the kind that hooks in the front. I began fumbling with the catch, deliberately stalling to see how Hal would react. To my surprise, he said, "Here, let me help you with that," and unsnapped it before I knew what was happening.

It was the first time I was ever topless out of doors. It was an odd feeling. At first, gooseflesh formed on my breasts, not because I was cold, but just because I felt kind of nervous. Without realizing it, I folded my arms across my chest and looked around. "What if someone comes along?" I asked.

"Not likely," Hal responded. "It's the middle of the week. All the honest people are working. Come on, we're here to walk. Let's get going." With that, he started up the trail again, and I stepped along beside him.

After a few minutes, the nervousness left me, and I really began to enjoy the sunshine on my naked breasts. "I can understand why some people practice nudism," I said to Hal. "This really feels good."

"Yeah," Hal answered, watching my boobs jiggle. "And it's great to be able to see you. Hey," he added, "What would you think if I took off my walking shorts?"

The idea seemed so naughty that I liked it at once. "It's all right with me," I answered. "But only if I can, too." We giggled like a couple of teenagers, both of us excited about the idea of doing something so unconventional.

"What the hell," Hal said with a grin. "Let's both do it. What could be more natural?" As he spoke, he peeled off his shorts. His penis stirred a bit, becoming semi-erect.

"You're not fooling me for one minute," I said, pretending to scold him. "Being natural has nothing to do with it. You're just a dirty old man."

The truth was I was eager to be naked, too. With shaking fingers, I undid the buttons on my shorts and stepped out of them. For a moment I considered walking in my panties, but the expression of sexual hunger on Hal's face encouraged me to go all the way. He was looking friskier than I'd seen him in quite a few years, and I liked it.

"Would you like me to carry your clothes for you?" Hal asked, devouring me with his eyes.

"Let's be real daring," I suggested, my voice dropping almost to a whisper. "Let's leave our clothes here under a rock or something. We can pick them up on the way back."

My husband looked uncertain, but only for an instant. His eyes took on a gleam that would have done a teenager proud. "Right," he said. His penis sprang to full erection.

After stashing our clothes, we began walking arm in arm, but it was obvious we weren't going to get very far. Hal's stiff organ bounced up and down with every step, and my thighs were becoming moist. The breeze caressed my naked nipples until they pointed our way like beacons. Hal's hand slipped from my waist to stroke playfully at my backside.

"I like the feel of your ass muscles when you walk," he murmured, slipping his fingertips between my buttocks to pet lightly at my sensitive tissues.

Turning to him, I put my arms around his neck and pressed my breasts against his hairy chest. "Make love to me," I demanded, getting right to the point.

Taking me by the hand, Hal led me off the trail into a clump of trees. The foliage wouldn't have been thick enough to give us any privacy if there had been anyone around, but somehow it felt a little safer than the trail. I don't think either of us cared, anyway. We were as horny as a couple of youngsters and couldn't think of much besides our lust. I felt freer than I had ever felt before. And more aroused.

Stopping by the stump of a tree that had been cut down ages ago, we embraced again. I put one foot on the tree stump and leaned slightly forward, inviting my husband to enter me from behind. I could feel the smooth skin of his organ grazing my inner thighs as he searched for my opening.

Then he was in it. It was just the tip, nudging gently at my sex. Bending over a bit farther, I moved my legs to open myself for him. My excitement was wetting me, easing the friction of his penetration. Tentatively at first, and then surer of himself, he plunged forward, burying his length inside my vagina.

I bucked back at him, swallowing him deep within me. I could feel the sun and air caressing me as he drove in and out. He placed one hand on my hip to guide me against his hard thrusts. His other hand explored my breasts, playing with their flesh and tweaking my nipples.

We humped hard and fast, as we had in our younger days. Each time he rocked forward, I threw myself back at him, feeling his swinging scrotum slap against the backs of my thighs. He was like an adolescent, filled with sexual energy, capable of going on forever, filling me with his strength until I was totally satisfied.

I don't know how long we kept at it, but I do know that neither of us felt any need to hurry. After every few strokes, one of us would change position slightly, just enough to bring different parts of our bodies into contact. He was probing me in places where I was sure he had never been before. When I felt my orgasm coming, it was with no sense of the frantic urgency that usually heralds a climax. I was comfortable and content.

"Oh, Hal," I sighed. "I'm going to come."

"Yes, Donna," he answered. "I've been waiting for you."

I felt him thrash hard against me as we began the dizzy whirl through orgasm. The trees and sky and sun and air were all part of our erotic flight. The rocks and leaves seemed to be coming with us. It was glorious, one of the most glorious moments of my life.

Afterward, we stood for a long time, hugging and kissing each other under a canopy of oak leaves. Then, slowly, casually, we strolled back to where we had left our clothes. The world was ours. We were its only inhabitants. There wasn't another soul in the universe.

We dressed leisurely, reluctant to separate our skin from the sun and air. I tucked my breasts into the cups of my bra and slipped lazily into my shirt. Just as I began closing the first button, we heard voices. I looked up to see four young hikers walking down the road from the direction of the parking lot.

"Good afternoon," one of them called, as they went marching briskly by.

"Great day," Hal answered, tossing a friendly wave. When they were out of sight, he looked at me and smiled.

"We just made it," I said. Together, we burst into breathless laughter.

I don't ever remember having so much fun. I know we never had more exciting sex. I hope we get to do something like that again sometime. We can't plan it, though. It will have to be something that just happens.

BALLING ON THE COURT

Alan is five-foot-ten with a lean athletic body. Without making obvious efforts to do so, he manages to maintain a youthful appearance that belies his fifty-one years. His silver hair is carefully styled to cover an expanding bald spot. His green eyes sparkle in a face that is tanned by frequent outdoor activities. Although he holds a Ph.D. in chemistry, Alan works as sales manager for a major pharmaceutical company. He says that the best sex he ever had happened on a tennis court with a woman half his age.

♥   ♥   ♥

Barbara and I were married for more than twenty years. Our sex was okay, but never really great. I didn't mind, because I always had a girl or two on the side. In retrospect, I realize that I was a terrible husband. At some level, my wife always knew I was fooling around with other women, but she closed her eyes to it. Sex was never that important to her, anyway. She was more interested in our affluent lifestyle.

Everything changed when I got involved with Diane. She's not much more than half my age, but she's absolutely the most exciting creature I ever met.

When I started going out with her, it was just for sex, as with all the women I dated. Before I knew it, I was head over heels in love with her, or maybe just obsessed with her. Sometimes it's hard to tell the difference. I didn't mean for it to happen, but it did. Once I started seeing her, I didn't want any other women.

That's what broke up my marriage. As long as my affairs were casual, Barbara never mentioned them. When she found out about Diane, though, she refused to tolerate it. I'm sure Diane's age was a problem for Barbara, but what bothered her most was the fact that I wasn't going out with anyone else. That made my relationship with Diane serious. That's when Barbara filed for divorce. Except for a few financial problems, I didn't mind the divorce at all. It gave me more time for Diane.

I think what makes Diane so sexy is that she's completely uninhibited. When I'm out with her, I never know where or when we're going to end up doing it. She doesn't plan it. She just has such a spontaneous nature that she is willing to take advantage of whatever situation arises. I love the adventures that we have together. We've had sex at the most unusual times and places you can imagine. I guess the best time of all was one night on the tennis court.

Actually, tennis has been a kind of background for our entire relationship. The first time I saw her was at the tennis club. I go there a couple of times a week with some guys from work. We've been playing doubles together for years. I like tennis because it helps me stay fit, but also because I'm a bit of a dirty old man.

I love watching the women in their short skirts, especially when they bend over to pick up the balls. Women's underwear has always had an especially arousing effect on me. I think that's probably true of most men my age. As we were growing up, there wasn't any *Playboy* or *Penthouse* magazine with pictures of naked women. The best we could do was the Sunday supplement with its ads for bras and panties. I remember looking at those models posed primly in their cotton briefs and jerking off till my elbows were sore. To this day, I get stirred up by the slightest glimpse of a woman's undies.

I realize, of course, that the briefs women wear under their tennis skirts aren't really underwear at all. They're just like running shorts, only briefer. In fact, they wear panties underneath them. Nevertheless, when a woman bends over and her skirt rises up to reveal those little tennis bloomers, I can't help getting aroused. Sometimes I am so distracted that I'm lucky I don't get hit in the eye with a ball. My tennis buddies all kid me about it, but that doesn't stop me.

One afternoon, we were playing when Diane caught my eye. She was serving the ball on the next court, poised on her toes with her arms held high, causing the hem of her skirt to rise dangerously. Only a blind man would have failed to notice her.

She was about five-foot-three and wore her dark brown hair long and flowing. She had a tight little body, with pointy tits and the sweetest ass I ever saw. Her muscular legs were perfectly proportioned, all shapely curves even in her flatbottomed tennis shoes.

Her outfit was the standard white, but her skirt was shorter than usual. She must have had it taken up deliberately. I found myself staring openly, waiting for her to bend down so I could steal a peek at what she had on underneath. When it happened, my mouth dropped open. She wasn't wearing regulation tennis briefs. She had panties on, skimpy white lace panties. They were cut so high that they barely covered her in front and left most of her ass cheeks exposed.

When my friends saw what I was looking at, our game came to a temporary halt. For once, they joined me in staring rather than ribbing me about it. Silently, we watched her play. When she bent over, one of the other guys groaned. She must have heard him but acted as if she didn't. It was obvious that she enjoyed putting on a show.

After that, we hit the ball around a bit longer, but none of us was interested in keeping score. When she left the court, there didn't seem to be much point in our staying, so our game ended early. The other guys wanted to stand around and talk about her and her sexy costume, but I had more important things to do. I knew I had to meet her.

I showered and dressed in record time so that I could be waiting for her when she came out of the women's locker room. As soon as she did, I went into action. Falling into step beside her, I said, "You know, I don't think we've ever met before, and I'd like to introduce myself."

She smiled. "I was wondering how long it would take for you to get around to me," she said matter-of-factly. "Sure I'll have a drink with you."

"I don't remember asking," I said, liking her at once. "My memory must be slipping."

"Yes," she said, her blue eyes flashing. "I have that effect on lots of men."

We rode in my car to a cocktail lounge near the tennis club and spent a couple of hours there getting to know each other. Diane was twenty-seven and an art dealer with a small but expensive uptown gallery. Right up front I told her I was married, but she just laughed. She said that made me safe and she liked that. We arranged to have dinner together the next night.

When I arrived at her apartment to pick her up, she was dressed and ready, but she invited me in for a drink. As she poured, I looked around her living room. Everything was expensive.

The paintings on the walls all had erotic themes. In one of them, a nude woman was looking in a mirror while caressing her own breasts. Her pose and the expression she was wearing captured my attention. I found myself becoming mildly aroused as I studied it.

"Do you like that one?" Diane asked, handing me a glass.

"Yes," I said. "It's very erotic."

"I agree," she answered softly. "It's one of my favorites. Every time I look at it, I get turned on."

"I'm glad to hear you say that," I admitted. "Because it has that effect on me, too. I wasn't sure that was a legitimate response to art."

"Of course it's legitimate," she answered. "Did that painting give you an erection?"

I was a little startled by her directness but not the least displeased. "Yes, I guess it did," I confessed.

"Let me see," she said, stepping in front of me and patting the crotch of my pants with the palm of her hand. My penis twitched against her. Swiftly, she pulled down my zipper and extracted my swelling organ. I was taken completely by surprise.

She clawed at me, pulling off my clothes and filling her hands with my sexual hardware. Within seconds, she was on her back on the floor with her skirt up and her legs apart, tugging me down on top of her. Without any foreplay, I was in her. I thrust only eight or nine times before I started to come. Her cries began just as mine were subsiding. Afterward, as we rearranged our clothing, I said, "Wow, that was a nice surprise. Most women prefer to do it *after* dinner."

"Maybe we'll do it after dinner, too," she answered. "That depends on how we feel then. But I felt like doing it now."

"Do you always do it whenever you feel like it?" I asked.

"I believe in taking advantage of the moment," she replied. *"Carpe diem!* Seize the day."

In the months that have followed, I found out that she actually lives that philosophy. We have sex at the drop of a hat, any time and any place that the mood strikes her. When we are in bed in her apartment, it might go on for hours. But when we grab a surprise quickie in some unanticipated situation, the two of us can come and be dressed again within seconds. She never ceases to astound me.

That's probably what makes her so attractive to me. At my age, everything had started to take on the aspect of a routine. Diane has changed all that. With her, nothing is predictable. Sometimes she'll act in a way which is totally conventional, and a moment later she'll do something totally unexpected. I'd say she's like a child, except that when it comes to making love, she's all woman. The result is that since I met Diane, I just don't have a need for other women anymore.

I think the best sex we ever had was on the tennis court. We were both working late and had agreed to meet at the tennis club at nine for a quick game. The club keeps the lights on until ten, so that would give us an hour to play. Lots of other people had the same idea, because when we started, every court was in use.

After warming up for a few minutes, we volleyed for the serve. Every now and then I deliberately hit the ball into the fence so that she'd have to bend down to pick it up. By now I knew that Diane always wore lacy panties when playing tennis. That gave the game a whole new dimension for me. Instead of putting my imagination to work on those white nylon bloomers that women usually wear on the court, I got to watch Diane show me her lingerie.

Fifteen minutes into the game, I was so turned on that I thought I might trip over my hard-on while chasing the balls. Each time Diane stood up after bending over, she looked at me and said something like, "Did you like that?" Once she even kicked the ball against the net so that when she picked it up I could have a close-up view of her scantily covered bottom.

I was just about to serve the ball when everything went dark. Frustrated grumbles could be heard from the other courts, where players were complaining about the interruption of their games. There wasn't a light to be seen, not even in the clubhouse. A voice shouted, "Power failure, folks. Just stay where you are. We'll have the lights on again in a few moments."

I walked toward the net, cautious until my eyes slowly became accustomed to the dark. When they did, I saw Diane facing me from her side of the net and wearing an impish grin. She was holding her skirt up above her waist. Her panties lay on the court surface next to her. She had removed them in the dark and was showing me her nakedness. I knew it was an invitation.

I vaulted the net and put my arms around her. Diane fumbled with the waistband of my shorts, stripping them from me and casting them, with my underwear, into a pile beside her panties. Lifting her skirt again, she began rubbing the hair of her pubis against my swollen erection.

"Hey," I said. "The lights can go on again at any minute. And we're not the only people here."

Diane lifted herself up to wrap her legs around my waist. "Then we'd better be quick," she murmured, lowering herself to take me inside her.

When she began a rhythmic rolling motion with her pelvis, I stopped worrying about the lights and let my dick do the thinking. Her soft wetness enveloped me completely. At that moment, it was all that mattered. I cupped her naked buttocks in my hands to move her up and down the length of my erection.

At first, the spontaneity of our union excited me the way it usually does when Diane's lack of inhibition takes me by surprise. As I drove in and out of her, though, I realized that there was something extra special about this time. If the lights went on, we would be on display. The possibility inflamed us both.

She was whispering ferocious obscenities in my ear, whipping me up to a sexual frenzy. I thrust hard and deep against her, plunging into the whirlpool of her sex. We were racing to a swift climax, caught up in the moment and not caring about the time. "Come in me," she commanded. "Come in me now!"

Her words sent me spinning into space, and I began spewing immediately. When I started pumping, her orgasm struck. Her thighs pressed tight against me, her contractions matching mine. Together we spiraled, seized violently by a tornado of passion. Within seconds, we reached its summit and began the floating descent that returned us to the world.

As our mutual climax wound down, Diane's legs released their grip on my hips. We stood in fevered embrace, her arms still around my neck and my hands still clutching her ass. Our tongues were clashing in afterplay kisses when the lights suddenly went on. I was aware of it at once, even though my eyes were closed.

Realizing that I was bare assed, I tried to break the clinch, but Diane held on to me a moment longer. Sure that all the other tennis players were looking at us, I kept my eyes shut so I wouldn't have to face them. When Diane's arms relaxed, loosening their grasp, I stepped back against the net. I glanced quickly around, but everyone else on the courts seemed to be studiously looking elsewhere. Trying to use Diane as a shield, I hurried into my togs, thrusting her discarded panties into my pocket.

I couldn't wait to get off the court and away from the embarrassing situation. Once we were in the car, though, we laughed about it. I recalled the excitement much more than the embarrassment. Diane said she was proud of me, that I had more guts than a kid of twenty.

Nobody at the tennis club ever mentioned the incident, so I'll never know for sure whether anybody saw us or not. To tell you the truth, I don't really care. Life is for living, and it doesn't pay to worry about what other people think. To hell with them.

Leisurely lovemaking, the kind that goes on all night and builds slowly to a poetic climax, is wonderful. But great experiences don't all have to be like that. They can take place in a fleeting instant. Even though it happened in a flash, Diane's spontaneity made that minute on the tennis court the best sex I ever had.

I'm still seeing Diane. We might even get married someday. If we feel like it, that is, and if the moment's right. In the meantime, I've adopted her philosophy: *Carpe diem!*

THE MATINEE

Sheila, a charming, voluptuous woman of forty-one, usually keeps her long brown hair tied back to prevent it from falling in front of her dark eyes as she works in her specially outfitted kitchen. She operates a successful business at home, baking pies for many local restaurants. When her husband, Dave, is not delivering the pies, he assists her in the kitchen. At a height of five-foot-four, Sheila is about twenty-five pounds overweight, hiding the excess flesh under a loose-fitting dress. There is a chuckle in her voice when she exclaims, "Never trust a skinny baker!" Sheila says that the best sex she and Dave ever had took place unexpectedly one Sunday afternoon.

♥ ♥ ♥

I love working at home. It lets me spend lots of time with the kids. Dave and I have two teenagers. Millie's fifteen, and Tess is twelve. We just love them to death, but sometimes kids can really get on your nerves. That's what was happening that day.

It was a Sunday, just a few months ago. We work hard all week, sometimes for ten or eleven hours a day. Sunday is our day off. Usually we just hang around the house watching TV and relaxing. But this particular Sunday didn't feel like a day off at all.

For one thing, Millie had volunteered us to make cookies for a fundraiser at her high school, and we worked on them for most of the morning. Talk about a baker's holiday. Then Tess was whining about something or other and driving me absolutely nuts. When the last batch of cookies came out of the oven, I took off my apron and tossed it to Millie.

"All right," I said. "It's your project. You can clean up. Your daddy and I are going out for a while." Dave just stared at me without saying a word and followed me out the front door.

As soon as we were outside, he said, "Hey, babe, what was all that about? Where are we going?"

"I don't know," I told him. "I just needed to get away." I stood in the driveway for a moment, looking around. Then, because I couldn't think of anything else to do, I said, "Let's go to the supermarket. Not the one around the corner. Let's go to that fancy one across town. I could use a nice long walk."

"Sure, babe," Dave answered, falling into step beside me. "You're stressed. I can see it. A good walk will do us both some good."

We strode briskly for a few blocks, working off some of the steam that had been building. Then, feeling a bit more relaxed, I slowed our pace to a casual stroll. As we walked, I looked around at the neighborhood. We had reached a commercial district, and there were lots of interesting businesses lining the street.

I usually drive every place I go, concentrating on the road rather than the scenery. This was fun, especially since we hadn't planned it. "Look at all these stores," I said to Dave. "I didn't even know they were here."

We stopped for a moment to look into the window of an antiques shop, admiring the old clocks and knickknacks. The next place was a jewelry store, and I stood in front of it checking out the diamond rings. After a minute, Dave grabbed my arm and said, "Come on, let's keep walking."

"Relax," I answered sharply. "It doesn't cost anything to look. And anyway, it's safe. The place is closed on Sunday." I was just needling him. I wasn't really all that interested.

We picked up speed as we started walking again, but suddenly Dave stopped to stare into a shop that sold sexy lingerie. I stood next to him, paying more attention to him than to the stuff in the window. I got a kick out of the expression on his face as he looked at the lacy wisps that passed for bras and the little nothings they called panties.

"Like what you see?" I asked him.

He grinned, embarrassed. "I was just picturing you in some of that stuff," he said.

I noticed that he was getting kind of stiff in the pants. I knew very well that my big butt would never fit into those teeny G-strings, but I sure was glad Dave didn't see it that way.

Looking at the sexy undergarments in the window, I caught my reflection in the glass. I was wearing a shapeless flowered dress that hung on me like a sack. I was a sight. I had walked out of the house without a bra. In fact, I didn't even have any underpants on.

Dave was so busy studying the display of what they call "intimate apparel" that I doubt if he even noticed. I never knew him to be interested in window-shopping before. I practically had to drag him away from there.

I could see a movie theater in the middle of the next block. I didn't have any intention of going inside, but I always liked looking at the movie scenes in the still pictures they put up in front of a theater. I quickened my step, curious to see what was playing. When we got there, I was a little startled.

The theater certainly belonged on the same street as the lingerie shop. The marquee had four huge X's on it. The titles of the films they were showing were something like *Horny Sex Kittens* and *Lustful Appetites*. It was a porno theater.

I moved into the area next to the ticket booth to study the photos on display. In one of them, a woman with huge boobs was tied down spread-eagled on a bed. She was naked, but a little black rectangle had been colored in over her genitals. There were four naked men standing around the bed, also covered by black rectangles. One of them had a rectangle that reached almost to his knee. I studied the picture, wondering if his thing could really be that big.

Right alongside that one, another picture showed a woman sandwiched in between two men. One of the men had his back to the camera. No one had bothered to put a rectangle over his ass. I looked at it for a minute, thinking about the woman in the picture.

I couldn't exactly see what was happening, but I sure could imagine it. It looked like the men were filling both her openings at the same time. I found the thought deliciously exciting. I wondered whether the movie showed the scene in more explicit detail.

Dave began tugging at my arm. He looked kind of nervous. "Come on, babe," he said insistently. "I don't think this is the kind of place you want to be standing in front of. Let's get going." The soles of my shoes slipped on the pavement as he tried yanking me away from there.

Suddenly, I felt mischievous. "Wait a minute, Dave," I said. "Why don't you take me inside?" I was only kidding when I said it, but once the words were out, I realized that I did want to see what the movie was like.

"Are you nuts?" he asked, a look of disbelief on his face. "You can't go into a place like that. There are all sorts of perverts in there."

"So what?" I said. "I'll have you to protect me. Come on. I've never seen a porno movie. I'm dying to see what it's all about."

"Not now," he said, still trying to talk me out of it. "The kids are home waiting for us."

"Let 'em wait," I answered. "I'm not ready to go home yet. Come on, Dave. I dare you."

"I think you're serious," he said, laughing.

"You're damn right, I'm serious," I insisted. "I dare you, Dave. I dare you."

I watched Dave's expression change. He never could turn down a dare. Without another word, he dug some money out of his pocket and stepped up to the ticket window. "Two, please," he said. Waving the tickets in front of my face, he took my arm and led me inside.

When we walked in, there were images flickering across the screen, but the theater was so dark that I stumbled. "Here," Dave whispered hoarsely. "Let's just sit back here until our eyes get accustomed to the darkness."

I wanted to get closer to the screen, but Dave's suggestion seemed like a good one. We picked our way over a few seats until we reached the center of the last row. Suddenly, I felt a little nervous. Anxiously, I glanced around, trying to see whether there were any perverts sitting near us.

The place was practically empty. There were just a few people scattered here and there watching the screen. They were all men and they all looked pretty normal to me. Feeling a little more secure, I turned to look at the movie.

The timing was perfect. There on the screen was the sandwich scene from the picture outside. The woman was young—in her mid-twenties, I'd say. Somehow I had always figured that porno actresses were tired old hags. I was kind of surprised at how good-looking this one was.

The two men with her were helping her get undressed. She was already down to bra and panties. One of the men was standing behind her, unhooking her bra, while the other was tugging at the waistband of her panties. Her undergarments were lacy and brief. They looked like they could have come straight from the window Dave had been staring into just down the street. I must say that the sight of the two men removing those last bits of clothing from her body excited me.

When she was all naked, the camera moved in for a close-up, focusing first on her big boobs with their erect pink nipples. Then it panned down lower. Although she was a platinum blonde, the hair of her muff was dark brown. I wondered how she felt standing bare-assed naked for all the world to see.

The men were already undressed. The one who had been behind her had the biggest dick I ever saw. He must have been the man in the picture outside with the huge black rectangle over him. The other guy was pretty ample too, but nothing like his pal. They were standing next to a bed.

The one with the big dick lay down on his back on the bed. His hard-on stood straight up in the air like a flagpole. Without any ceremony, the girl got onto her knees, straddling him. The camera moved in for a close-up just in time to show him sliding slowly into her snatch. It seemed to go on forever. I just couldn't imagine any woman taking so much meat.

The other guy stood by the bed watching and stroking himself until he was rock hard. Then, as the girl moved rhythmically up and down on big-dick's rod, he got into position behind her. This time, the camera focused on her backside, filling the screen with the cheeks of her ass pumping away. Spreading her buttocks with one hand, he guided his organ toward her little brown hole.

I felt myself getting wet between the legs as I looked at two men's dicks at the same time. When the second one began penetrating her ass, I thought I would go up in smoke. I wondered what it felt like to be that woman. For a moment, I forgot where I was and who I was with, but the sound of Dave's heavy breathing brought me back.

Tearing my eyes from the screen, I glanced at my husband. He appeared to be in a trance, his mouth slightly open, his eyes glazed. I looked at his crotch and saw that his pants were stretched tight over his straining erection. Almost involuntarily, I reached for it. When my fingers closed around the taut material, I heard him gasp.

Without a second thought, I unzipped his fly. "Hey," he exploded in a hoarse whisper. "What the hell are you doing? Look where we are."

By now I had his hard-on out and was stroking it with my hand. "Shut up and enjoy it," I murmured, turning back to watch the movie. I had never done anything like this before and I was loving it.

Dave stopped protesting, his excitement overpowering his paranoia. I just kept rubbing him up and down while I watched the screen breathlessly. The woman was groaning at the double penetration, and I could almost feel it happening to me.

Suddenly, I did something I never thought I would do in a million years. Rising out of my seat, I sat on my husband's lap with my back against his chest so that we were both facing the screen. I arranged the skirt of my dress so that it covered us both, and I moved my hips, trying to impale myself on his swollen erection. I was so wet with excitement that it slid right in.

I felt Dave's hands creeping into the armholes of my dress until he had both my breasts cupped in his palms. He twirled my hard nipples in his fingers and rocked his pelvis up against me to drive himself all the way in. I humped up and down on him, trying to match our movements to the threesome on the screen.

I looked around the theater, unable to believe that I was actually doing a thing like this. I was so aroused that it gave me this weird courage. I didn't even try to hold back my cries as I felt an orgasm coming over me. It's a good thing the threesome in the movie were making enough noise to drown me out, because at that point I didn't care who heard me.

A second after I started to come, I felt Dave throbbing inside me. I could tell by the way he was squeezing my tits that he was coming with me. A few moments later, I was back in my own seat, primly smoothing my skirt over my knees.

Dave doesn't usually come that fast, and I *never* do. Most of the time, it takes me forever to have an orgasm. But that afternoon in the movie theater I got off within seconds. I guess it was a combination of things: the strange surroundings, the people sitting just a few rows away, the sex scene going on before my eyes. Most of all, though, I think it was the fact that we did it without planning to. It was something that just happened, something totally unexpected.

We never experienced anything like that before. I hope we will again sometime. But for now, Dave and I agree it was the best sex we ever had.

4

MAKING BELIEVE

Wouldn't it be nice if there were magic carpets that could take us anywhere and allow us to do anything? In fact, every one of us has one—the imagination. For a person who is not afraid or ashamed to use it, imagination is a vehicle that can travel to places that are otherwise inaccessible.

Our imaginations begin to work almost as soon as we are born, providing us with nonstop fantasies that play continuously in some hidden recess of our minds. As children, most of us acted out these fantasies in games we called "house," "school," or "cowboys." When we wanted to do things that we were too young to actually do, we pretended or made believe.

In addition to entertaining us, these games served as important parts of our education, preparing us for the experiences of life by giving us an opportunity to preview them. Of course, our games of "house" never involved mortgage payments, we never flunked math when playing "school," and when other "cowboys" shot us we never died for long. That was the best thing about making believe. Things never happened unless we wanted them to.

Some people believe that adults should never lose sight of reality, that pretending is only for children.

These people are missing lots of fun. Others know that games of make-believe don't have to stop when childhood ends. They play "paint ball" or attend murder-mystery dinner theaters, simulating experiences in which no danger is deadly and all endings are happy ones.

The couples in this chapter learned to apply this technique to their sex lives. They say that they had their best sex ever when pretending to be in places and situations that fascinated them but in which they would never really want to find themselves. They permitted their imaginations to weave tapestries of fantasy and make-believe, which they rode like magic carpets to fabulous destinations. Perhaps their stories will give you the inspiration to climb onto your own magic carpet some night or afternoon and let your imagination take you on an erotic journey of your own.

IMAGINARY ORGY

Jared is thirty-seven years old, five-foot-nine, and weighs 165. His brown eyes are owlish behind black-framed glasses. Jared and his wife, Carrie, age thirty-two, are CPAs, each employed by a different firm. Jared says that he and Carrie had their best sex ever when they turned a dull party into a make-believe orgy.

♥ ♥ ♥

Carrie and I are both on the partnership track at the accounting firms we are with. That means that if we generate enough business and bill enough hours, we get to have our names on the letterhead some day, along with a million others. That makes going to parties and socializing with the right people just as much a part of our profession as giving tax advice.

Everyone who goes to these parties is in the same boat as we are. They'd all rather be somewhere else, but it's important to see and be seen. It's especially important to look affluent. They say nothing succeeds like success.

The men all wear Armanis. The women dress in low-cut Chanels. Those high-fashion outfits always offer a banquet of cleavage, and most of the women who wear them just love showing it off. As far as I'm concerned, without cleavage the whole thing would be terminally boring. Naturally, I can't help but look.

Carrie noticed and kidded me about it one night after we came home from a party given by her firm. "Your eyes must be really tired," she said. "After all, looking down the fronts of all those dresses is hard work."

"What are you talking about?" I protested, trying to sound innocent. I guess I was a little embarrassed being caught by my wife. "Looking down the front of what dresses?"

Carrie snorted derisively. "Come on," she taunted. "If you were any more obvious, someone would have called the Peeping Tom squad. Anyway, with all the flesh on display, I would wonder about the hormones of any male that didn't look."

When I realized that she didn't mind my roving eyes, I felt a whole lot more comfortable. "How can you blame me?" I asked. "The party was so dull that the stuff inside those dresses was the only interesting thing I saw all evening. Besides, you can really learn a lot about people that way."

"Really, now," Carrie said in a doubtful tone. "Arousing, maybe. But what the hell did you learn?"

"Oh, you'd be surprised," I told her. "Did you know, for example, that the office manager of your firm has a little butterfly tattooed on her right breast?"

Surprised wasn't a strong enough word. Carrie looked shocked. "You're kidding," she sputtered. "Judith has a tattoo? On her boob? I can't believe it. It's just too incongruous. She's so stuffy."

I was beginning to like this. "And Frank Wilson's wife," I continued. "You know who I mean. Old Pruneface? Would you believe she has the plumpest, hardest nipples you've ever seen. And they're the color of sweet pink bubblegum."

"You mean to tell me you get to see nipples!" she exclaimed. "Boy, when you look, you really look."

"It's all in knowing how," I bragged. "If you pick the right moment to peek—like when they're leaning forward to get up from the couch or bending over the coffee table for a drink—you can see it all. In the course of an evening, I get a bird's-eye view of maybe two dozen pairs of tits. Not counting yours."

The conversation was starting to get me aroused. Describing to my wife what I had seen and receiving her approval was strangely erotic. I could tell that my confession was having a similar effect on her. Carrie was undoing the buttons at the front of her dress, her face flushed with excitement. As she slipped the garment off her shoulders, her rose-colored nipples showed hard against the filmy material of her transparent bra.

"I don't think it's fair," she said in a tone of mock petulance. "You get to see all the women's boobs, but we poor women never get opportunities like that. Too bad men's fashions aren't as revealing as women's. I think I would enjoy parties more if I got a chance to peek at the men's dicks occasionally." The hoarse sound of her breathing told me how turned on she was.

Stepping behind her, I placed my hands on her shoulders and began stroking lightly over her bare skin with the tips of my fingers. I nuzzled the back of her neck, knowing that this always increased her heat. With practiced touch, I unhooked her bra, letting her ample breasts fall naturally from its confinement.

I cupped her soft firmness in both my hands. "I've seen some of those dicks in the locker room at the club," I whispered. "Would you like me to tell you about them?"

She turned her head to kiss me passionately on the lips. Our tongues touching sensuously, we shuffled toward the bedroom. "Did you ever see Frank Wilson naked?" she asked, a trace of embarrassment in her voice.

"Yes," I murmured. "You'd like looking at him, all right. He works out all the time and has a terrific body. He's got real big muscles with a dick to match. It's long and fat, with a huge round head shaped like a mushroom." To enhance her mounting excitement, I added, "It's humongous even when it's flaccid. I can just imagine how big it gets when he's using it on his prune-faced wife."

"Deirdre. Her name is Deirdre," Carrie giggled, pulling me down next to her on the bed. "Maybe Deirdre was thinking about her husband's stiff cock when you caught a glimpse of her nipples. Maybe that's why they were so big and hard." Her face took on a pensive look. Then, in a voice almost too soft for me to hear, she added, "Wouldn't it be fun if everybody came naked to these parties?"

The idea appealed to me. I said, "It would be even more fun if everybody was screwing instead of having those dull conversations."

Carrie sighed. The sound was familiar, but I usually didn't get to hear it except when we were making love. I realized that the fantasy was igniting her desire. "Who would you be screwing, Jared?" she asked.

"Why, I'd be screwing you, baby," I answered. "But wouldn't it be great to do it in a roomful of other people who are also doing it?"

Carrie, who had somehow managed to slip out of her dress, seized my hand and pressed it to her crotch. I could feel her heat through the fabric of her panties.

I moved my palm in little circles to bring her passion to a boil. When I stroked the damp material that clung to her flesh, I heard her sigh again.

"Tell me," she demanded in an aroused whisper. "Who would we see? What would they be doing?"

"Well," I began, my hand still petting her groin, "I'm sure Frank Wilson would be there with Pruneface. I can see them standing together next to the mantel. He's got a drink in his hand, but she's got his big dick in both of hers. She's stroking it slowly, making it harder and harder. Its bulbous head is turning purple. Deirdre's nipples are erect, the pink points jabbing at his bare chest. As he tips his head back to sip his martini, she drops to her knees and begins gobbling his hard-on."

I slipped my finger inside the crotch of my wife's panties and began sliding the tip up and down the length of her moistening slit. She kissed my ear, running her tongue all around it and taking most of it into her hot mouth. I couldn't remember ever seeing her get this excited this fast. "Look over there," I said, gesturing vaguely toward the other side of the room. "Who do you see and what are they doing?"

"I see Judith sprawled naked on the couch," Carrie began immediately. "Her legs are spread wide open so every detail of her sex is visible to anyone who wants to look. Her husband, Ned, is kissing her butterfly, the one she's got tattooed on her breast. Her nipples are standing straight out from the front of her tits. They're bright red, like a pair of bing cherries. He's sucking on one of them now. Listen, Jared. Can you hear her moans of pleasure?"

"Sure can," I answered, helping my wife out of her panties. "And so can Mr. Benjamin, the executive vice-president of your firm. Do you see him? He's standing next to the couch watching Ned and Judith while stroking his own cock. It's long and thin, and there's a little drop of moisture oozing out at the tip. Too bad he's a bachelor and has to jerk himself off."

"No," Carrie improvised. "Here comes Michelle, his secretary. She's always there to take care of his needs. Look. She's reaching out for his dick. There. She'll stroke it for him. That leaves his hands free to play with her ass."

"She's got a cute little ass, too," I threw in. "To go with her petite figure." As I spoke, my hands roamed freely over Carrie's naked body, stopping to tweak her nipples. Our sex talk had made them harder than ever before. I loved it.

"Tell me about Judith and Ned while I lick you," I said. "What are they doing now?" I touched my lips to the fountain of my wife's flowing womanhood. Her hips moved to raise her ass off the bed and press her mound against my face.

"There's a group of naked people standing around them," Carrie whispered, struggling to breathe evenly as my tongue probed her opening. "All the men have erections, and some of the women are stroking them. All eyes are on Judith and Ned. Judith is on the couch on her knees. She's bending over one of the sofa arms, waving her naked ass at Ned and the audience. Everyone can see the opening of her sex.

"Ned is on his knees behind her. As he moves forward to place the tip of his erection against her open slit, some of the people in the crowd are overcome with passion. I hear groans of pleasure and I'm not sure whether they are coming from Judith or from the people who are watching Ned enter her."

Carrie's body writhed uncontrollably each time the tip of my tongue found the throbbing button of her clitoris. For a moment she stopped talking, filling the air with the sound of her hoarse gasps. Then she continued in a seductive whisper.

"Ned's got his cock all the way inside his wife," Carrie said. "You can see his hard-on sliding easily in and out of her, and his balls slap against the backs of her thighs with every thrusting stroke." I never realized that my wife had such an explicit erotic imagination.

"The sight is turning everyone on," she continued. "Other couples are starting to do it, too. The Eastmans are trying to imitate Judith and Ned's position, only they're on the floor. Mrs. Eastman is on her hands and knees, and her husband is mounting her from behind. They are facing us and watching what you are doing to me."

The thought of performing for an audience aroused me even more, increasing the heat that coursed through my body as my mouth devoured my wife's vulva. My cock was so hard that it was starting to ache. I twisted to one side as if to show it to the couple who was ogling us from their position on the floor.

"Yes," Carrie hissed, her imagination in tune with mine. "Mrs. Eastman is staring at your hard-on. She can't take her eyes off it. I can't blame her, though. It's the biggest and best in the room." Her words were driving me wild.

"Mr. Eastman's eyes are glued to my tits," she murmured. "I hope you don't mind. I'm holding them in my hands to show them to him. I'm twisting my nipples with my fingers while your tongue sends chills through my body. Old Eastman is drooling at the sight of us. Now I'm cupping both breasts so he can get a really good look."

I know I wouldn't like it if anybody but me actually did get to see my wife's tits, but in fantasy, the idea was tremendously exciting. Taking my face from her heated sex, I said, "Open your legs wide. Let him see everything."

My words were like an electric shock going through Carrie. She moaned in passion and obliged me by parting her thighs to reveal herself to the imaginary eyes that were watching her. Tentatively at first, and then boldly, she began stroking her own sizzling tissues, putting on a hot sex show for the make-believe couples having sex all around us. Our fantasy game was getting to both of us.

"Put your cock between my tits," Carrie suggested. Holding her big breasts in her hands, she beckoned to me, inviting my hard-on to take its place in the cleft of her bosom. I stroked my dick with my hand, imagining that all eyes in the room had focused on us. Then, straddling my wife on my knees, I laid the length of my throbbing erection against the satiny smoothness of her skin.

Gently, Carrie pressed her breasts together, engulfing my swollen member in her sensuous flesh. Her nipples were practically touching each other. "Fuck me," she murmured. "Fuck my tits." Carrie didn't usually talk that way when we made love, but we were on a sexual high that left no room for inhibitions or embarrassment. "Fuck my tits while everybody watches us."

I pumped forward and back with my hips, plunging through the sweat-moistened softness of her bosom. My cock was throbbing with excitement, buried deep in the tunnel between her twin peaks. I could almost feel the stares of the other people at the party.

With my eyes closed, I saw them coupling in every possible position, on couches, chairs, the carpet, and even leaning against the walls. My field of fantasy vision was filled with cocks and asses and tits and vaginas and triangular patches of curling pubic hair.

The fabricated images had become so real to me that the room even seemed to smell of sex.

I realized that I was only an instant from spilling my come all over my wife's heaving bosom. Rearing back, I pulled myself away to savor the ecstatic moment a little longer. I wanted to be in her. I wanted to feel the warmth and pleasure of her inner membranes. I wanted everyone to watch as I penetrated my wife's tight wet pussy.

"Spread your legs," I whispered in her ear. "I'm going to fuck you now. In front of everyone."

With a sigh, Carrie lifted her legs high in the air and pulled them wide apart. "They're all looking at my pussy," she panted. "Put your cock in me and fuck me hard. Let them see how good a lover you are." Her words thrilled me, making my dick pulsate with hungry excitement.

Holding the base of my erection with my fingers, I guided its tip against her eager opening. Her vulva swallowed me up, its lubricated walls yielding slowly to the insistent pressure of my entry. She sucked me in deeper and deeper, like quicksand dragging its victim toward the center of the earth.

At last I felt my pubic bone collide with hers. My eyes were tightly closed. Our orgiastic fantasy was, for now, a total reality. I could hear the sounds of a dozen other people breathing lustfully as they made love all around us. I could feel their watchful gaze on our nude bodies as we cavorted savagely together.

Carrie was smashing and thrusting her pelvis hard against mine, meeting each of my potent drives with a burst of sexual energy. "I'm going to come," she announced, alerting the crowd of onlookers that her completion was fast approaching. "I'm going to flow like a river," she screamed, her excitement driving me to the edge of my own frenzied climax. "Oh, come with me," she commanded.

"Yes," I shouted. "I'm coming inside you. I'm coming now."

Her rhythmic gasps made it clear that her orgasm had begun just an instant before mine. I felt my cock pumping spurt after spurt of heated fluid deep into her channel to mingle with her own impassioned lovejuices. We seemed to come forever.

At first, I was acutely aware of the aroused audience watching our climb to fulfillment. Then I lost consciousness of everything but the orgasm itself. It was the strongest and most intense climax I ever experienced. Carrie's cries of passion said that the same was true for her.

After all our sexual energy was spent, we lay tangled in each other's arms, exhausted and completely satisfied. When I finally opened my eyes, I was almost surprised to see that we were alone. "Looks like everyone else went home," I said.

Carrie giggled. "Wasn't that the best ever?" she asked languidly.

"Absolutely," I answered.

As if reading from a script, we both added simultaneously, "That was the best sex I ever had."

And it was, too. I guess everybody, at some time in his or her life, dreams about going to a sex orgy. I don't think most people would ever really want to. I know I wouldn't. But fantasizing about it while making love allowed Carrie and me to experience it without actually doing it.

STRIPPING FOR ACTION

Marika, *twenty-seven, is a candidate for a Ph.D. in mathematics at one of America's finest universities. She looks more like a model than a mathematician, however, with a tall, shapely body and striking blond hair that hangs, soft and straight, almost to her waist. Her seductive hazel eyes gleam against the background of her creamy skin. Marika says that her best sex happened when she acted out one of her favorite fantasies soon after her husband, Alex, returned from a business trip.*

♥   ♥   ♥

Alex had been away at an engineering conference, and we hadn't seen each other for almost a week. As soon as he got home, I dragged him into the bedroom and jumped on his bones. Our lovemaking was hot and fast, both of us consumed by the need to satisfy our unfulfilled desires. Afterward, we lay together for the entire evening, talking and petting and making up for lost time.

Alex told me that the conference had consisted of a series of meetings and seminars that lasted from early morning right up until dinner every day. When I asked what he did after dinner, a mischievous smile crossed his face. "Well," he answered impishly. "One night I went to a strip show with some of the other guys. It was a hot one, too."

I was fascinated. I never admitted this to anyone before, but ever since I was a teenager, I fantasized about being a stripper in a nightclub filled with men. I guess being the center of erotic attention appeals to me. I remember, even as a young girl, I would love to walk on the beach in my teeniest bikini and feel the hungry stares of men trying to catch glimpses of my barely covered breasts or bottom.

For me, the thought of stripping onstage is the ultimate turn-on. All eyes would be on me, concentrating on every sensuous movement of my body. Nowadays I suppose such thoughts are regarded as un-feminist, but the idea of having a group of strange men get excited by watching me take off my clothes arouses me tremendously. It would make me feel like the sexiest woman in the world. No fantasy inflames me more than that one.

I wanted to hear more about Alex's night at the strip show. "Why don't you tell me about it?" I prompted. "What was it like? Give me all the explicit details."

Alex seemed nervous for a moment. "You're not jealous or anything, are you?" he asked solicitously.

"Heck, no," I said, my voice husky with excited curiosity. "I think it's sexy."

With a sigh of relief, he began. "Well, the place was called the Hot Box and it wasn't really much. It had a small stage surrounded by mirrors, and lots of little tables with chairs. My group was lucky enough to get one of the tables up front, right next to the stage."

"You mean lucky because that gave you a better view?" I asked.

"Well, sure," he said. "But the best part is that if a guy seated up front puts a tip on the table, the girl makes it part of her act to come up and do something special just for him. Like shaking her boobs in his face or something."

"Tell me about the girls," I asked. "How old were they? Were any of them my age?"

"Oh yeah," he answered, his eyes gleaming with remembered lust. "They ranged from their early twenties to early thirties, I'd say. And every one of them was good-looking. Some tall, some short, some with cute little titties, some with big bouncers. But all with great shapes."

My curiosity was increasing. "What did they do?" I asked breathlessly.

"When they're not dancing, they wait on tables, wearing real skimpy outfits," he explained. "Mostly just bras and panties. Then, when it's their turn to dance, they step into a little room to get ready, and they come out onstage."

"Do they wear striptease costumes?" I asked. "With feathers and stuff like that?"

"Most just wear regular clothes," Alex answered. "But real sexy. Like maybe a short denim skirt and bikini top. Usually each girl dances to three records. By the end of the first record, she's got all her clothes off except her underwear. They all wear little G-string panties and lacy bras."

I was becoming very aroused, picturing myself doing the things my husband was describing. I wanted to hear more, but I was afraid my voice would shake with excitement if I spoke. So I waited patiently for him to tell it in his own time.

"During the second record, the girl removes her bra and dances around showing off her bare breasts. I always like that part. Then, just before the record ends, she takes off her panties. At this point, the guys usually go wild, whistling and howling when she exposes her pussy. Lots of the men throw dollar bills on the stage. One of the girls had her pubic hair shaved into the shape of a heart. The guys must have tossed thirty or forty bucks at her when she took off her panties and showed that bush to them."

I felt like a spectator at a porno show.

"When the third record plays," he continued, "she dances and gyrates totally nude. During the dance, she'll lie on the floor and spread her legs wide to give everybody a good view of her open beaver. Or she'll lie back and throw her legs over her shoulders so they can see her ass, too."

I could see it in my mind as Alex talked about it. I would be naked while a hundred men cheered and threw money at me. In gratitude, I would open my thighs to reveal my most private places to them. I was getting hotter by the minute.

"There was one girl in particular," he went on. "She had big beautiful tits and thick cherry nipples. One of the boys in my group fell in love with her. He kept putting dollar bills on the table for her to come and pick up. Each time she did, she would get real close to him. Once, she put her foot up on the table so that her pussy was right in front of his face. He almost fell off his chair.

"After that, he laid a ten-dollar bill on the table. When she came over to get that one, she pressed her tits against his face for a long time. First she buried him in the valley between them. Then she shook slowly from side to side so that her nipples brushed across his nose and lips. Later that night, he went home with her."

"Really?" I asked, incredulous and captivated. "Are the girls hookers?"

"No," he answered. "I think it's really unusual for one of them to go out with a customer. It might even be illegal. She just must have really liked him. It was the last night, so I didn't get to talk to him and find out what happened. But I'm sure they spent the night screwing."

For a moment he fell wistfully silent. Then, in a soft voice, he mused, "You know, I've always fantasized about going home with one of those girls after the show. Not that I'd ever do it," he added hastily, as though fearful that I might need reassuring. "But I guess every man in the place imagines the same thing. After she dances for all the guys who paid the price of admission, she goes home and strips privately for me. I'm sure that in bed they're just like any other woman, but somehow there's a special sexy mystique about a stripper." He was silent for a moment, and then asked, "Does my little fantasy upset you?"

"No," I said in a sultry voice. "You're not the only one who has fantasies. Sometimes I imagine myself taking my clothes off and dancing nude in front of a group of men."

Our conversation was making me horny—so horny that I couldn't talk anymore. I just wanted to make love again. Shutting the light, I climbed on top of him. His penis was long and stiff, slipping easily into my lubricated vagina. Afterward, we both drifted off into a peaceful, satisfied sleep.

Alex left for work the next morning while I was still sleeping. I must have been dreaming about the things we discussed. The first thought I had when I woke up was a way to act out the fantasy that Alex and I had secretly shared.

By the time he came home from work, I was ready for him. I had set up a small table in the living room with a kitchen chair beside it. I greeted him at the door wearing cut-off jeans that showed the globes of my ass and a tank T-shirt that was two sizes too small for me. "Welcome to the Hot Box," I said, holding the door for him. "Right this way. Your table is waiting."

Alex looked my body up and down as I led him to the table. I loved the expression he wore. It was not that of a man looking at his wife. He stared at me, bewildered, as I placed a glass before him and poured beer from a bottle. Setting the bottle beside the glass, I said, "I'll collect for it later. It's my turn to dance."

Flipping a switch on the stereo, I began playing records that I had selected earlier that day. When Rod Stewart started singing "Hot legs, you're wearing me out," I went into my dance. At first a little embarrassed, I danced with my eyes closed. But as I began to imagine that I was being watched by a roomful of men, my embarrassment changed to excitement. I could feel my nipples getting hard under my clothes.

I opened my eyes and looked directly at Alex. He was staring at me as if seeing me for the first time. Pulling the tank top over my head, I removed it seductively. Alex hooted, making a catcall sound in a high raucous voice. "Yeah," he hollered. "Will you guys look at that!"

He seemed to know what I was thinking. Tossing the tank aside, I pictured a roomful of little tables, each with a cluster of horny men sitting around it. They were all admiring my body as I pranced around the room, arching my back to make the flesh of my breasts overflow the cups of my bra. I bumped and ground with my hips, caressing my own body lightly, running my hands over my bare belly and waist, stroking the bulging fabric of my bra with my palms, pinching my nipples where they tented the lacy material that barely covered them.

When my fingers undid the button at the top of my cut-offs, Alex whistled and stamped his feet. I displayed myself to one side of the room and then the other, imagining that dozens of men were staring in fascination as the descending zipper exposed a widening triangle of white lace panties. Turning my back, I began pushing the snug-fitting shorts down over my hips and buttocks.

By the time the first record was about over, I had slid the denim garment past my thighs and calves. As the music ended, I stepped out of the shorts and pirouetted slowly to show myself to Alex and the roomful of cheering men. Alex applauded and shouted, the sounds increasing my excitement. Standing, he threw a crumpled dollar bill onto the floor in front of me.

When I bent forward to pick up the tip, I knew that my breasts were spilling out of my bra, almost completely exposed. I could feel the gaze of men I didn't even know focusing on my burgeoning cleavage and staring at my partially bared bosom. I wanted them to see all of me.

Tina Turner began wailing the words to "Nutbush City," and I really threw myself into the dance. I thrust my pelvis forward and back in rhythm to the pounding tempo, aware that the dark shadow of my own "nut bush" was showing through the flimsy fabric of my panties. As soon as Alex hollered, "Show us your tits," I unsnapped the clasp at the front of my bra.

The undergarment fell open, its stuffed cups pulled apart by the dancing sway of my breasts. It remained in place, however, covering my bouncing globes. I rolled my pelvis in a circular motion, at the same time caressing my breasts with my hands through the material that shielded them from view. I drew back the lace, slowly revealing the smooth skin of my milky breasts and finally showing Alex and the boys the hard pink caps of my turgid nipples.

I was so aroused that I felt dampness seeping from my vulva to saturate the taut crotchband of the panties, which were all I had on. I turned my back to the audience and bent forward, peeking back at Alex from between my spread legs. I ran my fingers up my thighs until they were stroking lightly over the roundness of my bottom. As the record neared its end, I stood and turned to face Alex again, ready, at last, to draw the panties down and show off my heated passion place.

Noticing that Alex had placed a dollar bill on the edge of his table, I danced toward it, looking directly into his eyes and wiggling my fanny and shoulders in his direction. His sight was riveted to my swaying breasts as I moved closer and closer to where he sat. I could see the front of his pants stretching tight over his swollen organ.

With one hand, I took the proffered tip while, with the other, I stripped the panties from my body. Lifting the damp wisp of lace with my toe, I kicked it into my husband's lap. Alex hooted again, holding the panties against his face and moaning dramatically. I imagined that he was the envy of every man in the place.

I stepped back just as the third record started playing. When Mick Jagger's voice enunciated, "She's a honky-tonk woman," I dropped to the floor on my belly and lifted my backside high in the air. I knew that Alex and the other men could see not only my ass but also the reddened slit of my vagina peeking back at them. I felt the exciting impact of a wadded dollar bill striking my splayed buttocks.

Rolling onto my back, I raised my legs in the air, spreading them slowly to reveal the puckered lips of my sex. As I parted my thighs yet farther, I felt my heated womanhood opening to expose the pink inner membranes, now inflamed with my rising lust. With my hands, I touched my inner thighs, stroking my way to the edge of my bush and then running my fingers lightly through the curls.

When I saw Alex place a ten-dollar bill on the table in front of him, I realized that he wanted me. I had never dated a customer before, but there was something about this sexy stranger that really appealed to me. I knew nothing about him, but I had stripped and spread my legs for him. Now he was wildly hungry for my body. The game I was playing in my head turned me on even more.

He openly desired me. I knew his mind was filled with fantasies of taking me to bed after the show. Like all the other men in the room, he probably thought deep down that it was nothing more than an impossible dream. But I could make it come true for him.

I rose from the floor and danced toward the fascinated customer until my bare skin was only inches from his hungry eyes. With deliberate movements, I placed one foot on the edge of his table, bringing my sex so close to his face that he could feel its heat. I thrust forward and back with my hips, causing the puffy lips to open and close before his hypnotized gaze.

Taking the ten-dollar bill from the table, I stroked my body with it, tracing little circles around my nipples and trailing sensuous lines across my belly. Dragging it over my hairy mound, I nudged a corner of it lightly at my emerging clitoris. Alex groaned softly, and I knew that it was no act. My performance was obviously having a powerful effect on him. It looked like his trousers would burst from the pressure of his erection against the constraining cloth.

I wanted him as much as he wanted me. Without ceremony, I pulled him to his feet and quickly unzipped his pants, freeing his swollen member.

Stripping him from the waist down, I pushed him back into the chair and lowered myself onto his lap, facing him.

I stroked his face with my breasts, rotating my groin over his throbbing erection. I could feel the tip of his hard-on grazing the insides of my legs as it reached for the softness of my feminine opening. Flexing my knees, I lowered myself farther until he pressed hungrily against my moistly puckered membranes.

I felt him entering me, penetrating my vagina by exquisitely gradual degrees. At last I rested against his lap, his penis buried completely within me. His hands grasped my buttocks forcefully, rocking me up and down as his rigid organ pistoned furiously inside me. I wrapped my arms tightly around his neck and twined my legs around his waist.

Alex's muscles tightened as he rose to a standing position. My body was welded to his, our pelvises thrusting together in a frenzy of passion. My back undulated to drive his penis in and out of me with long, agonizingly gradual strokes. I felt the edge of the table against my buttocks and allowed Alex to place me gingerly on its surface. I reclined against the tabletop and unlocked my ankles. Lifting my legs in the air, I placed my heels against his shoulders to allow maximum penetration.

He thrust forward, plunging into the tunnel of my womanhood. The penetration was deeper and more forceful than any I had ever felt before. His testicles slapped against my upturned bottom each time he buried his probing organ within me. I felt the hairs of his scrotum tickling the sensitive tissues of my femininity.

I was rising to a stupendous climax. I wanted to hold it back, to keep the tension building as long as I possibly could. But I knew it was hopeless. I was being carried off on a wave of feeling that took complete control of my responses. I had no choice but to yield to an orgasm that threatened to tear my loins apart if I resisted any longer.

"Oh, God," I screamed. "Alex, I'm going to come."

My announcement took my husband over the top. I felt his semen gush into me the moment I articulated the erotic promise. At the same instant, my orgasm struck, drowning me in a whirling sea of ecstasy. Our juices merged as our bodies coupled on the little nightclub table. We bucked and thrust together until every drop had been drained from us.

Later, we found ourselves in bed, repeating the contact of our bodies. We moved about on the mattress, each of us straddling and riding the other before changing position to be straddled and ridden. We made love through the night until our exhaustion left us in a state of panting unconsciousness. In the morning, we made love again before our eyes were fully open.

Alex and I still talk about that wonderful night when I stripped for him and an imaginary audience. The weird mix of reality and fantasy held us both in thrall, maximizing our excitement. We agree that it was the best sex we ever had, but we both know that, as long as we are willing to act out each other's fantasies, there will be even better sex to come.

5

THE SWEET TORMENT OF ANTICIPATION

Christmas begins long before December 25. The excitement starts some time around Thanksgiving, when stores begin putting out their Christmas displays. A day or two later, carols can be heard in office-building elevators. Soon the nights are illuminated by flashing lights, and families take drives to sections of town where the holiday decorations are particularly elaborate.

Well in advance of the big day, we match people to gifts, compiling written or mental lists. We go to malls or out-of-the-way shops, where we finger the merchandise while imagining reactions to the purchases we are considering. By December 24, when the wrapped packages find their way under a tree, the excitement has been building for weeks.

To children, Christmas Eve is interminable and its excitement overwhelming. The youngest try to stay awake long enough to catch Santa dropping in with his bag full of goodies. Older siblings feign sophisticated amusement at their antics but watch the clock's apparently frozen minute hand in unbearable agony.

Imagine how much less fun it would be if we just popped into some government office on Christmas Day for our allotment of presents. Kids may complain about waiting, and adults may gripe about shopping, but few of us would be willing to give up those torments. If all the preparation was eliminated, most of the excitement would go with it.

No matter how painful it may seem, anticipation has a way of heightening pleasure. The time spent trying to guess what's in a certain package or envisioning the receiver's response to it helps increase the joy of giving and receiving. When the exchange actually occurs, everyone's excitement is so intensified that the wrappings seem more colorful and the ribbons all look brighter.

Some people have discovered that anticipation has the same effect on sexual experience. The hours or days that they spend planning and thinking about an impending erotic encounter become part of that encounter, stretching its pleasure out over an extended period. When the day or night of passion finally arrives, they feel every touch more acutely, they savor every scent or flavor more appreciatively. The couples in this chapter made the best of involuntary separations by indulging in the sweet torment of anticipation, saying that it led to the best sex they ever had.

WORTH WAITING FOR

Steffie is five-foot-ten and twenty-two years old. Her blond hair is cut short, but its mannish style does nothing to detract from her sensuous femininity. Her complexion is smooth and fair; her eyes are a soft green. Although she is slender, her ample bosom requires that she have her military uniforms altered to fit her properly. Steffie is a United States Marine who works in the public relations division as a writer for the base newsletter. Her husband, Ed, twenty-four, is also a Marine. Steffie says that the best sex she and Ed ever had was on the night he returned from the war in the Persian Gulf.

♥ ♥ ♥

I joined the Marines to get out of Kansas. That was two years ago. I was just a kid. After basic, I was assigned to this base and went to work on the newsletter. It was here that I met Ed. He was two years older than I was, and the warmest, handsomest grunt I ever saw. We went out a few times, and then he asked me to marry him. I jumped at the chance.

I was a virgin when we got married, and Ed didn't have much experience himself. We sort of learned about sex together. I was very bashful about love-making at first. Ed was patient, but I knew that he hoped I'd become more spontaneous and less inhibited. He was always trying to perform oral sex on me, but I just didn't feel comfortable about it and wouldn't let him.

Just as we were settling in to our new life together, Ed got the word that he was shipping out. There was talk about the possibility of war in the Persian Gulf, but this was several months before the war actually started. I remember that I was angry when he told me about going, because the idea of running off to war made him excited and enthusiastic even though it meant leaving me behind. But being a Marine, it didn't take me too long to get used to the idea. After all, that's our job.

The night before he left for the Gulf, we were both feeling depressed about not seeing each other again for months. Neither of us talked about the possibility that there might really be a war and that we might never see each other again. I guess we both realized it without mentioning it.

When we went to bed, Ed took me in his arms and held my body close to his. We usually wore pajamas, but this night we were both naked. I suppose we expected our last night together to be filled with passion. It didn't turn out that way, though.

We both made an effort to get into it but never really pulled it off. We did manage to have sex, but it seemed to end as soon as it started. I had imagined long hours of lovemaking, but I guess our emotions made that impossible. Instead, we spent most of the night talking.

Ed left early the next morning. For the first week, his absence didn't really sink in. I was alone, but it felt as though he was off on a training exercise. After a while, I began to feel very lonely. Every day I wrote him about how things were on the base and how much I missed him. Once in a while he wrote me a few lines. I never expected more than that because Ed's not much of a writer.

Some of my friends told me that I was beginning to wear my loneliness on my face where everybody could see it. I didn't pay attention to them until one afternoon when I was eating lunch and Tom slipped into an empty chair at my table. As editor of the base newsletter, Tom was my supervisor. He had always been known as a woman chaser, but lately he had become even more flirtatious. Everyone said that with so many of the men away in the Gulf, Tom was making out with dozens of lonely women. He was more successful than he had ever been before.

"Hi, Steffie," Tom said. "You look like you're hurting, and I'll bet I know what the problem is." Before I had a chance to say anything, he put his arm across my shoulders and added, "You're not getting enough sex. That would make any girl feel lousy. And to a sexy woman like you, it must be absolute hell."

Even though Tom's touch felt good, I gently took his hand and removed his arm from around me. "I'll manage," I said.

"Why should you?" Tom asked with an air of mock concern. "You're a healthy young woman. That thing between your legs is going to dry up if you don't use it. And if you think you feel bad now, wait till that happens."

I knew that Tom was putting the make on me, but he had a way of speaking that made it hard for me to get angry with him. I found him more amusing than offensive. "I'll manage," I said again.

"Look," he said. "There are two things you can do about it. You can get yourself a vibrator, which is better than nothing, I suppose. Or you can have the real thing."

"And what would that be?" I asked, already knowing what his answer would be.

"Baby," he said. "You give me a chance, and I'll make you the most satisfied woman on earth. I'll stroke you and pet you all over until you're so wet and hot that you can't stand it anymore. But, don't worry, I won't make you beg. My timing is absolutely perfect. The instant you're ready, I'll ram my nine-incher so deep into you that you won't ever want the war to end."

"The war hasn't even started yet, Tom," I said. "And thanks for the offer, but I'm really not that desperate."

"That's okay," Tom answered with a wink as he rose from the table. "You know where to reach me if you do get desperate enough. In the meantime, you'd better think about getting that vibrator."

I chuckled, but Tom's words had a discomforting effect on me. Later, as I sat working at my desk, I thought about how good it would feel to have a nine-incher deep inside me. But the only man I was interested in was Ed, and he was thousands of miles away. That night as I lay in bed alone, I imagined making love to Ed. The tingling itch of unsatisfied desire kept me tossing and turning until the sun came up.

About a week later, I decided to buy a vibrator. I had never actually seen one, and I wasn't sure of how it was supposed to be used. I remembered once seeing an ad for vibrators in one of Ed's magazines, and so I started turning pages. The magazine was filled with pictures of pretty girls in the nude. I knew that Ed sometimes got aroused looking at these pictures and, in the condition I was in, I even found myself becoming aroused.

By the time I located the vibrator ad, I wanted to have it immediately. I called the 800 number and gave the woman at the other end my credit-card information. At her suggestion, I agreed to pay extra for next-day delivery.

The following day when I saw the express package in my mailbox, I grabbed it and carried it into my apartment with a feeling of mixed excitement and uncertainty. I stared at the package for a moment, wondering what to do with it. Then I tore it open.

The vibrator was shaped like an erect penis and was covered with soft pink latex that was warm and smooth to the touch. I couldn't get over how real it looked and felt. It reminded me so much of Eddie's that I was getting excited just holding it. Feeling a rush of heat enveloping my loins, I went into the bedroom, undressed, and lay down on the bed.

Believe it or not, I had never masturbated before. I had never even touched myself down there except when I was using the bathroom or bathing. I felt awkward holding the vibrator in my hand. The only thing I could think of doing with it was putting it inside me as though it were Eddie's penis.

I was wet, and the vibrator slid in easily. It felt so good going in that it made me remember how long it had been since I was with Eddie. Clumsily, I began moving it in and out, trying to imitate the motions of intercourse. I felt my excitement building. Then I remembered that it was supposed to vibrate. I felt around with my fingertip until I found a little switch at its base. When I flipped it on, it began to hum, and the vibrations intensified the erotic sensation.

I continued prodding myself with the humming instrument, sliding it in and out of me. I was shocked at how quickly it brought me to the edge of orgasm. It felt too good to come to an end. Hoping to prolong the delightful tingling, I pulled the vibrator out of me and began stroking it lightly around the moist lips of my opening. It seemed that the closer I brought it to the top of my slit, the better it felt. Suddenly, I bumped it against the little button that nestled among the folds of flesh, and I shuddered.

I knew about the clit, of course. I had always known that it was there and I had always been aware that it was extremely sensitive. But I don't think it had ever been stimulated directly before. When the vibrator touched it, it seemed to swell like a balloon, and I was overwhelmed with an intense rush. Gently I placed the vibrating tip against it.

I felt that I couldn't catch my breath. I was overpowered with a sense of extreme heat. When it happened, I came so hard that I think I must have screamed. I squeezed my eyes shut, but there were bright lights flashing inside the lids. As my orgasm reached a peak, I found myself imagining Ed's tongue stroking my clit.

Afterward, as I lay naked on the bed, I thought regretfully about all the times that Ed wanted to lick me and I wouldn't let him. Although it was just a mechanical device, the vibrator had introduced me to the wonderfully sensitive response built in to my little love button. It was obvious that a warm, wet, human tongue stroking and sucking on it would feel even better. How ironic that I had discovered this new pleasure while Ed was away and unable to enjoy it with me. I resolved to share my erotic delight with him through letters.

The next day at lunch I told my secret to Judy, the newsletter's photographer. Judy was my very best friend and confidante. When I described the vibrator to her, she giggled. "I've been using one for a long time," she said. "I'm not as lucky as you. I'm not married. I got my vibrator years ago."

THE BEST SEX I EVER HAD

I told Judy that I wanted to write a letter to Ed telling him about my new discovery. I wanted to make the letter sexy so that it would get Ed real horny. Judy grinned impishly. "Why don't you put in a few photos of yourself?" she asked slyly. "Naked, I mean. Let him see what he's missing."

I thought of the pictures of nude women I had seen while looking for the vibrator ad. "Well, I don't know," I said. "He can see much prettier girls than me in magazines. I'd be willing to send him pictures of me, but I'd want them to be different. Special."

Judy grinned again. "How about some pictures of you playing with your new toy?" she suggested. "That ought to turn him on."

I felt my pulse quicken. "Now, that's a great idea," I said. Then my face fell. "But how would I take pictures like that?"

"That's what friends are for," Judy answered. "I'll take them for you."

The idea was exciting but embarrassing at the same time. Until the previous night, I had never even touched myself, and now I was thinking about posing lewdly with a vibrator in front of Judy and her camera. Oh, but what one does for love.

That evening, Judy came home with me and set up her equipment in my bedroom. She began taking pictures of me while I was undressing. As I think back on it, I realize that it was really a lot of fun. And a very sexy experience. I took off one garment at a time, posing in my bra and panties, and then just in my panties. When Judy told me to remove them, I hesitated for a moment.

Although I had often taken showers in the presence of other women, it felt weird to be deliberately exposing my pussy that way while Judy watched and took pictures. I was acutely conscious of my curling blond pubic hair and the swollen pink lips of my sex. When Judy directed me to lie back on the bed and spread my thighs, I blushingly obeyed her.

She continued to snap photos of my nakedness from every possible angle. Then she said, "Now the vibrator shots." As the camera clicked away, I followed Judy's instructions, touching my erect nipple with it, inserting the artificial penis inside me, and stroking my outer lips and clit with it.

The next day when Judy presented me with the prints, I was shocked. The photos were the sexiest I had ever seen. Too dirty even for a magazine. "Boy," I thought. "Will these pictures ever turn Eddie on."

That night, I wrote Eddie a long, hot letter. Instead of including the usual chitchat about life on the base, I went right into a description of what I would want him to do if he were there with me right then. I said that I wished he could be in the room with me watching as I got undressed, then touching and stroking me all over my naked body. I enclosed some of the photos that Judy had taken while I was removing my clothes, creating a series that began with me in full uniform and ended with me wearing nothing but panties pulled about halfway down my legs.

A few days later, I wrote Eddie another letter filled with even more explicit descriptions. I accompanied this one with photos of me lying naked on the bed with my legs spread wide so that he could see every detail of my pussy. I said that I could imagine him putting his fingers in me and even kissing me down there with his hot mouth. I realized that the letter and photos might be seen by military censors, but by now I had become so horny that somehow the idea aroused me even more. I got so excited by the thought of Eddie kissing my pussy that as soon as I was finished writing, I rushed into the bedroom and went to bed with my vibrator.

As I slid it around the mouth of my sex and slipped it slowly and teasingly inside me, I thought about Eddie and about the nights of passion that we would have when he came home. I was so aroused by these thoughts that my flesh was soon throbbing to the rhythms of climax. When it was done, I reread my letter and found myself becoming aroused all over again by descriptions of the pleasures that lay ahead.

In my next love letter I enclosed the last of the lewd photos. In some of these, the pink vibrator was driven deep into me. In others, I was holding its tip against the swollen nub of my clit. I knew that the sight would inflame Eddie's passion, no matter where he was and no matter what was happening. It certainly inflamed mine.

In the letter itself, I said that I longed to feel Eddie's tongue licking my clit and probing inside me. I could just imagine Eddie's face as he read my descriptions of his mouth against my pussy, of his lips and tongue nibbling my sensitive membranes—things I never used to let him do. I could imagine his excitement as he looked at the pictures of me doing lewd and lustful things to myself while I awaited his return.

This kind of writing was quite unlike me. But my longing and wanting for him was driving me to do things I had never done before. My dreams about the joys we would have when he got home turned me into a creature of lust, burying my embarrassment where it couldn't interfere with our desire. Anticipating the nights of delight that lay ahead of us kept me going as I waited for his return. I hoped it would have the same effect on him.

I wrote to him regularly, describing the things we would do together and referring to the photos, which

I hoped he was carrying with him day and night. He wrote to me also, making clumsy but endearing attempts to duplicate my erotic descriptions. Even though his words were frequently misspelled and often misused, the crudeness of his images was brutally exciting and increased the ardor of my anticipation.

When war broke out, I knew that the mail wasn't getting through consistently, but I kept writing. I felt that my letters would keep him safe. Somehow I thought that his expectations would give him a stronger reason to survive combat, and I was sure that the erotic images that my words and pictures conjured would keep him alert and on his toes.

Finally, just a few months after it began, the war ended. At first I was disappointed by the news that it might still be several months before all the troops returned. As it turned out, however, Eddie's group was one of the first to come home because it had been one of the first to be shipped out. At last I got the word that they would be home within a week. A few days later Tom told me that Eddie would be arriving that very night. When he said I could leave early to go home and get ready, I practically flew from the base to my apartment.

I ran into the bedroom, stripped off my uniform, and jumped into the shower. After drying myself with a towel, I applied perfume all over my body, making sure to use a little extra between my breasts and on my curling sex hair. I put on a sexy pair of brief pink bikini panties and a matching bra that was not much more than a wisp of soft fabric that did little to hold my heavy breasts in place. My heart beating with anticipation, I slipped into jeans and a sweater so tight that my erect nipples could be seen straining against it. All I could think about was getting my hands on Ed.

When I arrived at the base airport, a large crowd of people was already waiting for the air transport. Although I knew lots of the other women who were there, we hardly spoke to one another. I was in my own little world of sexual anticipation. As I look back on it, I guess most of the others were thinking the same sort of things I was. We had all been without our men for months.

I don't remember much about the landing or Eddie's arrival. All I know is that the moment he got off the plane, he swept me up in his arms and we rushed back to our apartment. When we got inside, Eddie kissed me hard on the lips while he unzipped my pants. Within seconds, my sweater and jeans lay in a heap, and his fingers were working at the snaps of my bra. When it was off, we both fell to the floor. He struggled for a moment with my panties before ripping them off in a desperation of hunger.

"Oh, those letters," he whispered. "And the pictures. I haven't been able to think of anything else for months."

I felt his thick penis bumping at my pussy as he thrust forward like an animal. I was about to guide him in with my hands when he found the mark unassisted. In a flash, his big organ was inside me, driving in to the hilt and filling me with passion. I moaned without inhibition as he rode in and out of me. He was so hungry, he came at once.

We lay together embracing each other as he panted and strained to catch his breath. "I missed you so much," he murmured, his lips nuzzling my ear. "I'm so glad to be here with you like this. I want to make love to you until the world ends."

He began kissing my lips passionately, his tongue stroking my teeth. My desire increased as he slowly nibbled and kissed my throat, working his way toward the tops of my heaving breasts. My nipples were so erect that they ached as he took first one and then the other in his mouth, licking gently at first and then sucking harder.

He kissed circles around my pink aureoles, licking the curves of my breasts until I was tingling all over. Then, slowly, he began trailing his tongue across my stomach, dipping lightly into the crater of my navel. The juices of my sex were flowing freely.

"I thought of nothing but this," I heard him murmur as he nibbled his way down through my tangled nest of pubic hair. Then I felt the first contact of his tongue with my clit. It was like a wonderful electric shock, causing my whole body to jerk with sweet anticipation.

He licked slowly, tracing little figure eights around the erect button. Occasionally, just when I thought I couldn't stand it anymore, he dipped lower, stroking the lips of my opening with the flat of his tongue and tasting the spicy juices of my arousal. Then he returned to my clit, sucking hungrily at it. It was everything I had imagined and more. I had anticipated this very moment, and now it was upon me.

I felt myself building to the greatest climax of my life. It was exquisite. It was magnificent. It was more intense than the vibrator and more exciting than anything I had ever hoped for. I started to sob as the sweet waves of pleasure began to roll through my groin.

"Oh, Eddie," I cried. "Oh, Eddie. Yes. Yes. Oh, Eddie, I love you." The orgasm was beginning now, and my pelvis was rocking wildly. My back arched as I raised my hips, pressing my sex even tighter against his mouth and tongue. I lost all consciousness, surrendering to pure pleasure. I had never experienced anything like this before. It was stupendous. I floated on a cloud until all my passion was used up. Then I just lay there, basking in the glow.

Eddie lay beside me, holding me in his arms. Then, rising from the floor, he lifted me and carried me to the bedroom, where he placed me gently on the bed. "I've been dreaming about this for so long," he said, "that I had to begin by relieving the pressure. Now we can take our time and really make love."

I felt him growing hard again as he pressed himself tightly against me, and I knew our night of love was just beginning. The months that we had spent imagining and anticipating our reunion had prepared us for total excitement and complete ecstasy. We had missed each other terribly, and neither of us would ever want to go through a period of separation like that again. But the night of Eddie's return gave us both the best sex we ever had.

DISCOVERIES

♥ ♥ ♥

At thirty, Lou is the owner
of his own bicycle shop, having parlayed a college sport
into an occupation. He is five-foot-eight, with a lithe and
muscular body that gives the impression, an accurate one,
of great strength. His eyes are brown and his sandy hair
is fashionably styled. Lou looks up from a wheel that he is
straightening to tell us about his most erotic experience.

♥ ♥ ♥

Tracy and I practically grew
up together. Her family moved into the house next
door to mine when we were in the fifth grade. She
was a cutie at the age of eleven, built like a boy but
wearing frilly girl clothes. My mom said that it would
be nice if I walked her to school on her first day and
introduced her to the other kids. So I did. After that,
we became the best of friends.

Tracy and I were in the same class throughout
grammar school and junior high school. Most of
the guys I knew had other guys for best friends,
and most of the girls had other girls. But Tracy
and I had each other. We did everything together. We studied together, we joined the same clubs
at school, we were even co-stars in the school
play.

When we weren't with each other, we would talk on the telephone for hours. We told each other everything. I remember when Tracy had her first period. She told me before she even told her mother.

Tracy started going out with boys and I started going out with girls when we were in high school. Naturally, we told each other all about our dates in explicit detail. At first the conversations were about where we went, with whom, what we did, what movies we saw. As we began to discover sex, we talked about that, too.

I remember telling Tracy about the first time a girl let me touch her breasts. I was so excited, I thought I had finally arrived at the gates of heaven. Tracy knew the girl. "Ooh, she's got big ones," she said. "I wish I had boobs that size. Did she let you put your hand inside her bra?"

Somehow it seemed perfectly natural for her to be asking me questions like that, and I was completely comfortable answering them. I told her how exciting it was to feel the girl's nipples get hard when I touched them and how I was hoping that on the next date I would be able to see them, maybe even suck on them.

"Last night I went out with Bobby," she said. "And he wanted to feel my titties."

"Did you let him?" I asked, breathless with curiosity.

"No," she said, adding thoughtfully, "but I think I will at the drive-in tomorrow night. After all, I don't want you getting too far ahead of me."

A couple of years later, Tracy told me that she finally had sexual intercourse. We were juniors in high school. She had been dating a college sophomore. She said he made her feel that if she didn't do it with him it would mean that she was still a child. She confessed that the actual screwing didn't feel all that good because it was over so fast, but the best part was when he licked her right before getting on top of her.

I was fascinated. I had heard of girls giving guys blowjobs, but it never occurred to me that a guy might do the same thing to a girl. After Tracy described how good it felt when he put his tongue inside her and all around her opening, I was dying to try it myself.

There was a girl named Ginger that all the guys said would do it with anybody. As soon as I got off the phone with Tracy, I called Ginger and asked her out. She said that her parents were away for the evening and invited me to come to her house. I practically ran.

The minute I knocked, Ginger pulled the door open and began kissing me. Within minutes we were both naked, and Ginger was lying back on the couch with her legs spread wide. I just stood there staring, my eyes riveted to her crotch. I was mesmerized by the delicate pink slit with its thick pouting lips nestling in the midst of that hairy jungle.

Falling to my knees beside the couch, I clumsily started kissing and licking her moist tissues. I was a real klutz, unsure of my movements, afraid that my lack of experience would show. After a few minutes, though, I started to experiment, discovering ways to make Ginger groan and sigh. Strange as it seemed, I found myself imagining that I was with Tracy.

Eventually, I mounted Ginger and thrust myself inside her. My first experience at intercourse was a lot like Tracy's. It was over too fast for me to feel anything. When we were done, all I really wanted to do was rush off and get to a phone so I could tell Tracy about it.

Tracy had a million and one questions. What did it taste like? What did it feel like? How did Ginger act while I was doing it? I described the whole episode to Tracy. I think that my conversation with her actually turned out to be more exciting than the things I had done with Ginger.

After high school, Tracy and I went away to colleges at different ends of the country. Even though we couldn't afford to talk on the phone as much as we used to, we stayed in touch by card and letter. We remained as close as ever, continuing to share our experiences.

I called her a few weeks before our first Christmas vacation, and we talked for a while about our classes and that sort of thing. As usual, the conversation turned to more intimate matters. I started telling her about a girl I had been seeing, but when I got to the sex part, I found myself becoming uncomfortable. I just couldn't bring myself to discuss the explicit details the way I always had. And Tracy didn't seem to be asking her usual questions.

When she told me about a guy she was dating, she seemed to be selecting her words rather carefully. It was obvious that she had been to bed with him, but she wasn't saying much about it, and I wasn't asking. In fact, without even thinking, I mumbled something about a paper that was due the next morning and hurried off the phone.

That night I just couldn't get to sleep. I lay in bed for hours, thinking about our conversation. I was imagining Tracy with another guy. I could see them in bed together, naked, rolling in each other's arms. The images were so horrible that they made me sick to my stomach. I couldn't understand why I was feeling this way. It wasn't until the morning light began creeping through my window that I realized I was jealous. The reason I was jealous was that I was in love with Tracy.

Suddenly, I understood that I had been in love with her ever since we were eleven. I was too dumb, too stupid, too blind to recognize it until now. I felt like I had been struck between the eyes with a sledge-hammer. I was stunned.

At first I didn't know what to do about it. Tracy was my best friend. I always told her everything. I wanted to call her immediately and tell her about my discovery, but I was afraid. If she didn't feel the same way, would this be the end of our friendship?

It was risky, but I had no choice. Now that the feeling was out, I'd never be able to contain it. It was only six A.M. but I reached for the phone. Tracy answered on the first ring.

"I'm sorry," I said. "Did I wake you?"

"No," she replied with no trace of sleep in her voice. "I've been up all night."

"Me, too," I said. Then, taking a deep breath, I blurted out everything I was feeling. Frightened of what she might say, I kept talking as fast as I could until I had to stop for a breath. When I did, I heard Tracy laughing.

"I love you, too," she said at last. "Why did it take us this long to figure it out? Are we the stupidest people in the world, or what?"

We must have talked for an hour, babbling on about our feelings for each other. I never felt better in my life. The sky was blue, the sun was shining, the whole world was wonderful.

We spoke on the phone again that night. And the next night. And the night after that. All we could think about was Christmas vacation, less than three weeks away. We were both going home and we would be together at last. In one of our conversations, Tracy said, "Do you realize we've known each other since we were kids and we've never even kissed?"

When she said it, something suddenly dawned on me. Ever since the morning when I discovered how I felt about her, my head had been in the clouds. I had been thinking abstractly, my mind filled with rosy thoughts of love and eternity. The concept was so new that sharing these thoughts seemed like an end in itself. But Tracy's words brought me back to earth. In a few weeks I would be seeing her, holding her, kissing her. We would be making love. The thought excited me more than anything ever had before.

"Tracy," I murmured. "I can't wait to feel my lips against yours. I can't wait to taste your breath."

"I want to feel your hands on my body," she said, her voice trembling with excitement.

For a few moments, we were silent, both of us imagining the things we would discover together. Then, in a tentative whisper, Tracy said, "Lou, tell me what you're going to do to me."

I remembered our high school conversation about the night she lost her virginity. I remembered how disappointed she was that it was over so quickly and how excited it made her to talk about oral sex. "I'm going to take my time," I said. "I'm going to lick you until you beg me to stop."

Her soft sensual sigh induced me to go on. "I want to put my tongue inside you and slowly explore you with my mouth. I'll kiss and nibble your most sensitive places while you tell me the parts you like best. I want you to teach me how to please you like nobody ever has."

"Yes," she said. "I want us to do things together that neither one of us has ever done before."

The next night we talked about oral sex again. Nervously, I admitted that I had never tried sixty-nine. I was fearful that she would tell me that she had done it with someone else and that, if she did, my jealousy

141

would be overwhelming. I was relieved when she said, "You mean both of us doing it at the same time. Oooh, I've always wanted to try that."

We talked about it for hours, imagining together how it would feel when we finally got to do it. I described the position I had always fantasized about. I would lie on my back while she straddled me above. Her knees would be on either side of my head; her face would hover over my groin. She would lower herself slowly so that my mouth came into contact with her sex at the same moment that her mouth came into contact with mine.

Our conversation was so hot I'm surprised the wires didn't burn. At one point I noticed something peculiar about the sound of Tracy's breathing. "Do you know what I'm doing right now?" she asked.

I thought I did, but I said, "No. Tell me."

"Well," she said breathlessly, "I've got my finger right where I want you to put your tongue. And I'm rubbing myself slowly and lightly, just the way I want you to lick me."

As she spoke, I began stroking myself, too. At first I just listened to her description of the way she was masturbating, allowing it to lift me to higher and higher levels of excitement. Then, when I felt that I was about to burst, I said, "Oh, Tracy, I'm doing it, too. I'm holding my cock and imagining that it's your hand on me. I think I'm going to come."

"Yes," she gasped. "Yes. But wait for me. Just another moment. Wait. Wait. Yes, oh yes. Yes, I'm going to come with you. Now. Yes, now."

Her words and the excitement in her voice carried me over the top. I closed my eyes at the moment I pumped my juices into the air. I pictured her hand around my cock, her mouth and tongue caressing my throbbing organ. I don't know what excited me more:

my orgasm or the image of her body writhing as her groans announced her climax.

After that, we had sex on the telephone at least once a day, sometimes more often. Although our Christmas vacation was getting nearer and nearer, I thought we would die of anticipation. Our long-distance love-making was stupendous, but we both knew that the real thing would be even more sensational.

That last week before the break was ecstatic torment. We talked every morning and again every night. In between, I sneaked off to the bathroom four or five times a day to jerk off. I never felt completely satisfied.

Neither of us was willing to wait any longer than necessary for our dreamed-of reunion. Tracy and I agreed to meet at the airport, telling our parents that we would be arriving a day later than we actually were. My plane came in about an hour before Tracy's, so when she got there I had already made arrangements for a night at a nearby hotel.

I drove us there in a rented car. It was a good thing there wasn't any traffic, because I couldn't concentrate on driving. In fact, I couldn't think about anything other than getting into that room with her. The hotel clerk worked so slowly that I wanted to jump over the counter and strangle him. Finally, though, we got our key and headed for the elevator.

If we had the elevator to ourselves, I think we would have made love on the way up. As it was, a family with enough luggage for a lifetime rode up with us, and we had to restrain ourselves until we were in the room. Once inside, we fell upon each other like a pair of hungry animals.

The desire that had been building inside us for the last ten years got the better of us. We literally tore each other's clothes off, tossing the tattered garments around us as we kissed and grabbed at each other. I bit her nipples and squeezed her breasts until she squealed. She pulled so hard on my cock that it hurt me. But neither of us stopped or wanted the other to stop—not for a second.

We sank to the floor, making frantic love on the carpet without a thought for the slow acts we had been discussing on the phone. All I wanted was to be inside her. All she wanted was to envelop me in her softness. We hardly moved before our cries signaled our sudden, simultaneous orgasm. Afterward, we lay panting and gasping for breath, our arms tightly wound around each other's bodies.

A few minutes later, we began to make love again. This time we moved more slowly, each taking the time to explore the other with the loving curiosity that had been driving us. I kissed her nipples and stroked her soft white belly, while she ran her fingers over my chest and thighs.

Lifting her, I rose from the floor and carried her to the bed, laying her gently across it. I stood for a moment, looking down at her glorious nudity, barely able to comprehend that she was mine, all mine at last. I felt tears flowing from my eyes and realized that she was also crying. Our mutual joy was overwhelming us. Slowly, I bent over her, burying my face between her thighs to sip the honey of her loving excitement.

As I began licking her, I felt her hands on my buttocks. She nudged me gently, guiding me down onto the mattress beside her, rolling me onto my back. At the same time, she moved into position above me, straddling me the way we had imagined and described in our telephone conversations.

I gazed up at her open vagina, its pink lips dotted with glistening diamonds of moisture. Slowly, tantalizingly, she lowered it toward my face. I could smell the fragrance of her as the space between us narrowed. When she was only a centimeter away from me, I thrust my tongue outward, stroking it lightly over her delicately parted lips. At that same moment, I felt the warm wetness of her mouth closing around the swollen tip of my pulsating penis.

So slowly that the progress was almost imperceptible, she took me into her mouth. Following her lead, I slid my tongue gently between the membranes of her vulva. For what seemed like a century, we remained poised that way, tasting the spice of each other's desire. Each of us slowly became accustomed to the delectable feel of the other's oral explorations; each savored the taste of the other's genital secretions.

Our contact was so wonderful, so fulfilling, so exciting, that it was like the first time for both of us. We licked and sucked each other until we came to the brink of mutual climax. Then, as if by agreement, we retreated far enough down the slope to allow us to climb slowly to the peak once again. We continued pressing our mouths to each other's genitals long into the night, each of us recalling the erotic descriptions that had inflamed our imaginations during our daily and nightly telephone conversations.

We had so long anticipated this moment that neither of us wanted it to end. We drew it out for as long as we possibly could until both of us felt as though we would shatter if we did not allow our orgasms to release themselves. Then, each of us knowing instinctively when the other was ready, we let it happen.

Our anticipation had prepared us for something spectacular, but it was even better than we had imagined. We sobbed together as the throes of our climax rocked the bed and filled the air with the scent of our passions. We kept making oral love until we drifted off on a cloud of contentment. Lying side by side, we reveled in our union.

That night of our first sexual encounter was the best we ever had. I guess the build-up created by our explicit sex talk and the longing that we finally recognized as true love enhanced our fulfillment and increased the rewards we both felt. We spent the rest of the night trying to do all the other things we had discussed and envisioned, but we realized at last that one night would not be sufficient. We would have a lifetime to spend learning to please and delight each other.

The following semester, I transferred to Tracy's college so that we would never have to be apart again. A year later we were married, and now we are living happily ever after. Sometimes during the day, we talk to each other on the phone about the sex games we're going to play in the evening. That little taste of anticipation always sparks our sexual appetites.

6

THE ELEMENT
OF SURPRISE

Sometimes the business of life can become humdrum. We tend to wake up at the same time every morning and go to bed at the same time every night. We build our lives around our sleep, our work, and our meals. If we ever stop to smell the proverbial roses, we are likely to do so only while waiting for the daily commuter train, or during some unexpected free moment in our scheduled routine.

That is probably why almost everybody loves a surprise. Most of us have delightful memories of the special surprises we received as children on our birthdays or at Christmas. Even in our tender years, we appreciated anything sufficiently out of the ordinary to excite us with a break from routine.

For many adults, sex becomes part of life's routine. It is scheduled, like a meal, to follow the eleven o'clock news on Mondays and Saturdays, or to precede the kids' return from a scout meeting on Wednesday evenings. As a result, it loses some of the sparkle that it had when it was a fresh, new experience.

Some couples have learned to recapture that sparkle by surprising each other with an occasional gift of sex. For the person who receives such a gift, a childlike feeling of excitement lights up the adult world.

For the giver, there is the secret pleasure that comes from planning a surprise and looking forward to that special moment when the secret can be revealed and mutually enjoyed.

The element of surprise made a real difference in the lives of both couples described in this chapter. They discovered that having sex at unexpected times and in unusual settings put a new vitality in their relationships. The excitement that they felt when surprising or being surprised by a partner carried over to spice up even their routine sexual moments.

A GIFT OF SEX

*L*eslie *is a petite woman in
her late thirties. Her brown hair is soft and shoulder length.
Her blue eyes sparkle in a way that suggests a childlike love of good times and fun. Leslie holds a middle-
management position in a nationwide corporation. Her husband, Rob, is a civil engineer. Leslie says that the best
sex they ever had was the gift that she gave Rob on his
thirty-fifth birthday.*

♥   ♥   ♥

Rob and I had been married
for ten years, and we always had a pretty good sex
life. Actually, in the beginning it was fantastic. We
made love almost every night and sometimes in the
middle of the day on weekends. Then, after a few
years, we both got sort of involved in our work until
we found we spent more time on it than on anything
else in our lives. When we were home, we were both
usually pretty tired. And being the parents of two
young daughters took a lot out of us.

It got to the point where we were having sex only
once or twice a week. Well, most of the time, I guess
it was more like once a week than twice. We both
enjoyed it, but the truth is that sex didn't seem all

that important to either of us anymore. We probably would have gone on that way forever if it hadn't been for a TV talk show that I saw one afternoon when I stayed home with the flu.

The subject was how to keep the spark alive in marriage. One of the women on the show said that she had taken belly-dancing lessons so that she could arouse her husband with sexy entertainment. I was only half interested and wasn't listening very closely until I heard another woman say that she and her husband liked to surprise each other with gifts of sex. That really captured my attention! I was intrigued, wondering exactly how they did that. You know how television is, though. They talk about sex quite openly, but then never really give you any details.

I thought about it for days afterward and became extremely aroused by the idea. Rob's birthday was only a few weeks away, and I had been planning to buy him something for his desk. But how exciting it would be if I could surprise him with a gift of sex. I racked my brain trying to figure out what to do. One day I was returning to my office from lunch when I noticed a porno shop. You know, one of those places that sell X-rated videos and products they call "marital aids."

Even though I had passed that little store hundreds of times, I had never given it a thought before. Now, although I didn't quite know what I had in mind, it occurred to me that I might find something in a shop like that to help me with Rob's birthday surprise. For a moment, I asked myself, "Should I or shouldn't I?" Then, before I had time to answer my own question, I brazenly walked inside.

It was amazing. The place was like an erotic supermarket. There were quite a few people browsing, and

I was kind of surprised to see that they all looked respectable. Each corner of the store was filled with different kinds of erotic objects. I didn't know where to look first. I was drawn to a rack of lingerie. Certainly, a gift of sex would have to begin with a sexy costume.

Ordinarily, I am a conservative dresser, even down to my underwear, which is expensive but usually sensible. The seductive undergarments on display were far from conservative, but I was fascinated by them. I imagined wearing them for Rob and was surprised to find that the thought of parading before him in what I considered to be the attire of a hooker excited me tremendously.

There were so many sexy outfits to choose from that I was somewhat intimidated. But I soon got over that and started looking through them just as though I were in a department store. I'm real petite and don't usually have much to choose from. But in this store, there were dozens of styles in my size. I decided to pick something red to set off my dark brown hair. To my own amazement, I selected a sheer red peek-a-boo bra with nipple cutouts and matching panties with an open crotch. The seductive openings were trimmed in lace, and I flushed as I imagined it framing the parts that my underwear usually covers. Deep down I didn't believe that I would really buy or wear garments like that. Other women might, but not me. The whole idea was too kinky. Yet for some reason, I set them aside and continued looking through the lingerie until I found a lacy black garter belt and black fish-net stockings.

I placed the red and black wisps of fabric next to each other and tried to picture how they would look on me. Suddenly, I realized that I *could* go through with it, that it *wasn't* all that kinky for me to dress in a way that was designed to turn on my husband. The whole idea of giving Rob a surprise gift of sex began to seem very real to me. I resolved to buy the lingerie and anything else I could find that would help turn his birthday into an erotic event.

When I left the porno shop, I was carrying a large bag containing my purchases. In addition to the undergarments, I had bought an X-rated videotape, a tube of strawberry-flavored lipstick, and products called Sex Oil, Harem Incense, and Seduction Candles. Later that day, I picked up an expensive bottle of red wine and two cans of smoked oysters, because I had heard that the combination could increase sexual stamina. I hadn't been so excited about anything in a long time.

After that, planning Rob's erotic surprise occupied my thoughts day and night. My excitement increased until his birthday finally arrived. I arranged to send the kids to their grandma's for the night and left work early so that I would have time to get everything together. I wanted to turn our living room into a passion palace. Since we always made love in the bedroom, I thought the change would add to the surprise.

I started a fire in the fireplace and set Seduction Candles on every flat surface. The flickering light gave the room a sexy ambience, and the scent of burning incense added to the mood. I glanced about, enjoying the warm and seductive atmosphere that I had created. I felt stimulated just thinking about the night I had planned. I poured two glasses of wine and set them on the cocktail table next to a plate of smoked oysters.

We have a big-screen TV and a videocassette recorder in our living room. I popped the X-rated tape into the VCR and let it run past the credits. The film opened with a man and woman sitting in bed with their clothes on. The woman was telling the man that she was hungry for sex. Suddenly, she began to undress, and he did the same. Within moments, they were kissing and touching each other all over. It aroused me to watch them.

I decided it was time to put on the sexy outfit I had bought. Shutting off the VCR, I went into the bedroom and laid my new undergarments on the bed. As I removed my clothes, I had a deliciously naughty feeling. When I was naked, I looked into the mirror at my own breasts and hips. I know my body is far from perfect, but at that moment I felt like the sexiest woman in the world. I was unabashedly setting out to seduce my own husband, and the thought made me feel wonderful.

Slowly, I slipped into the red crotchless panties, adjusting the lacy opening so that Rob wouldn't realize it was there until I showed it to him. Then I put on the bra, garter belt, and hose. My skin glowed white against the lacy fabrics of red and black. I got a pair of black pumps out of my closet and stepped into them. Looking into the mirror again, I appraised myself from top to bottom.

My body was firm and tight, and I knew that I looked good in the brief erotic garments. I had worn sexy lingerie on a few occasions in the past, but certainly nothing like this. It made me feel like a different person. I thought about how aroused Rob would get when he walked in the door to find me wearing those seductive things. The idea made me even more excited.

I could see my nipples hardening, standing out through the lace-trimmed openings in the bra. I stared at them for a moment, watching them become even more erect under my own gaze. I wished that they were darker so that they would be sure to catch his eye. Then, remembering the strawberry lipstick, I wondered how my nipples would look if I applied a little of it to them. My breasts were beginning to tingle at the thought. When I touched the rigid pink buds with the tip of the lipstick, I felt a pleasurable sensation flash all the way through my body.

At that moment, I heard Rob's car pulling into the driveway. I took a quick look in the mirror at my rouged nipples and the red lace that framed them and rushed back into the living room to make sure everything was ready. I turned on the VCR just as Rob opened the door.

When he entered, he was bewildered by the unfamiliar lighting effects. Wearing a puzzled expression, he glanced around at the candles and at the porno scene playing on the big-screen TV, as if he thought that he might have walked into the wrong house. Then he saw me and noticed my provocative costume. He stared for a moment at my nipples poking through the lacy peek-a-boo openings. His eyes roamed my body appreciatively, lingering over the black garter belt and stockings. "What's all this?" he asked softly, obviously pleased by what he saw.

"Happy birthday," I said, approaching him slowly with my hips swaying. I wrapped my arms around his neck, kissing him on the mouth. Then, stepping back, I handed him a glass of wine.

"I can't believe all this," he murmured. "I can't believe this outfit you're wearing. I love it. You've never worn anything like this before. What's going on?"

Before answering, I began to unbutton his shirt with deliberate movements. As I did so, I realized that our lovemaking had become so routine that I couldn't remember the last time I had undressed him. When his shirt was open, I pulled it off him and began caressing his chest with my hands. I heard him sigh.

"It's your birthday present," I said. "It's a gift of sex. Relax and enjoy it. Taste the wine." He sipped tentatively, rolling the wine on his tongue to savor its subtle flavor, and sighed with pleasure. He sipped again, and as he did so, I began to unbuckle his belt.

Rob stood still as I unzipped his pants and slipped them down over his muscular legs until they fell to the floor. I could see his erection straining at the front of his shorts. Swiftly, I stripped them from him, leaving him completely naked. He was throbbing with excitement.

"The wine," I whispered. "Drink some more wine." As he sipped from his glass, I reached for the sex oil and poured a little of it onto the palm of my hand. Gently, I began stroking his erection, rubbing the scented oil into the smooth skin. I heard him draw in his breath sharply. I didn't usually play an aggressive role in our lovemaking and I was truly enjoying it. I liked the feeling of control it gave me to make his sex spring to the touch of my fingers.

He moaned. "If you don't stop now," he said, "it'll be all over."

"It won't be over," I said. "This is just the beginning. Don't hold back. Come whenever you want to. It's going to be a night you'll never forget."

The words had hardly left my lips when his penis began to swell and throb, and I knew that his orgasm was about to begin. "Go ahead, Rob," I crooned. "Let it happen. Let it flow." And it flowed. I felt his body tensing and relaxing repeatedly in the paroxysms of sexual climax. As his orgasm wound down, I led him toward the couch and eased him into it until we were sitting side by side.

After a moment, I reached for the plate of smoked oysters and placed one in his mouth. "Eat it," I whispered. "It's for sexual endurance." When he had swallowed it, I fed him another, and another. As he chewed them, we sipped wine and looked at the erotic acts taking place on the TV screen. Two couples were making love in the same bed, and the camera kept shifting from one to the other. Seeing the filmed close-ups of men's and women's sex organs fitting together was increasing my excitement and getting Rob started all over again.

I slid to my knees on the floor between his ankles and bent over his lap. His penis lay soft and shriveled in the tangled mat of curling pubic hair. I teased it lightly with the tip of my tongue and then took him into my mouth. When we first were married, I performed oral sex on him regularly, but for the past few years our sex had consisted of little more than penetration and thrusting. Tonight, though, I was giving him a gift. Tonight I would do everything I could think of to show him a good time!

At first I was afraid that I would be awkward, but as soon as I got started I felt like a sexual expert. I found myself enjoying the taste and the bulky heft of his manhood in my mouth. Within moments I was performing for my own pleasure as much as for his. Rob gasped, and I felt him beginning to harden again. I looked up at him and was thrilled to see that he was watching me intently. Almost without realizing what I was doing, I started putting on a show, making elaborate movements with my lips and tongue until I could feel him throbbing and pulsing.

Slowly, I let him slip from between my lips. His shaft was rigid and gleamed with moisture. Rising from the floor, I faced him and sat on his lap, straddling his thighs. I saw him looking at my painted nipples. "Taste them," I said. "It's part of the surprise."

He licked the tips of my breasts, smiling when he noticed the strawberry flavoring. I could feel the head of his manhood nudging at my opening through the fringed slit at the crotch of my sexy panties. Moving my hips slightly, I worked him inside. Then, with a forward thrust of my pelvis, I buried him completely. By now I was so wet that he slipped in easily. It felt wonderful.

The two of us rocked back and forth, undulating with rhythmic strokes that caused his length to slide in and out, warming and stretching my internal membranes. I felt him thickening and beginning to throb again. This time, I wanted to make it last. Withdrawing myself from his extended organ, I moved to the floor, falling to my hands and knees. With no trace of subtlety, I waved my backside at him, knowing that my wanton display would arouse him even further. With swaying movements, I silently invited him to enter me from behind.

We hadn't done it that way in years, but I had often fantasized about it, remembering the way he had mounted me "doggy-style" when we were first married. I guess I had been missing it without even knowing that I was. Back then I would sometimes remain poised that way for what seemed like hours as he slid forward slowly into me and rocked back even more slowly. To me, that position symbolized the leisurely lovemaking that we had been neglecting for so long. Somehow the freedom we had once known had been replaced by inhibitions.

Rob sat on the couch for a while watching me, obviously becoming even more aroused as he did so. Showing myself to him in that lewd and erotic way inflamed me also. I had not felt this uninhibited in years. What started as a gift for Rob was turning out to be a gift for me as well. Within moments, he was on his knees behind me, bumping my buttocks with his stiffness. Then he was in me, hunching wildly to bury his full length inside.

We moved together until we both came to the edge of explosion, and then, as if by mutual agreement, we held still for a while. I lowered my body until I lay flat on the floor with my breasts and belly pressed against the carpet. He waited a moment and then began a rhythmic thrusting again to carry us closer to climax. Reaching around me to cup my breasts in his hands, he stroked my nipples with his fingers. As he drove into me, I felt my orgasm approaching. When it struck, I moaned and sobbed in ecstasy. It was the most powerful sensation I had ever experienced. Before my climax ended, his began. Together, we drifted on a sea of sexual bliss.

That night we lay together for hours, hugging and kissing as we hadn't done in years. We stroked and petted each other's body until we were ready to make love again. Before the night ended, we experimented with every intercourse position that either of us could imagine, sometimes taking inspiration from the performance unfolding on the television screen. We both lost count of our orgasms.

We came to a new understanding about our sexuality. Like lots of other couples, we had become too absorbed in our work and in the minor problems of day-to-day life. As a result, we neglected our sexual needs for so long that we began to forget that we had them. The surprise gift of sex that I gave Rob that night was actually a gift that we gave each other, a gift that we gave our relationship.

We resolved not to make the same mistake again. We realized how important it was for us to find time to make love, and how exciting it was to bring a sense of surprise into our lives. Since then our sex life has improved tremendously. We often make love until the sun comes up. And we take every opportunity to surprise each other with gifts of sex. In fact, that surprise I planned for Rob on his thirty-fifth birthday turned out to be so important to us that we both agree that it was the best sex we ever had.

EXQUISITE DESSERT

$\mathbf{C}$*arl, thirty-three, is tall and brawny, carrying 210 pounds on his six-foot frame. His short hair is light brown like his eyes. When he moves, his muscles ripple impressively, muscles developed not from exercising in a gym, but from hard physical labor. Carl started working in construction when he was seventeen. For the past six years, he has owned his own contracting company. His twenty-six-year-old wife, Lucy, works as a sales representative for a women's clothing line. Carl says he and Lucy have their best sex when one plans an erotic surprise for the other.*

♥   ♥   ♥

Sex is always good for Lucy and me. I don't think it's ever going to get old with us. Probably one of the reasons for it is this little game we play. We love to surprise each other with unusual sex. Lucy started it all about six years ago. It was just after I got into my own business.

We were doing some subcontracting on a tall building that was being constructed in the center of town. One afternoon, just before quitting time, Johnnie, one of my workers, told me that there was a problem on the top floor. He asked me to go up and have a look with him. Now remember, this wasn't a building yet;

162

just the skeleton of a structure. You know, steel girders and poured concrete floors. Not much more.

I followed Johnnie into the cage—the construction
elevator. I punched the button for the thirty-seventh
floor. Then, just as the cage started going up, Johnnie
jumped off, hollering that he'd see me later. I couldn't
imagine what the hell was going on, but with that
elevator, once you punch in the floor number you
can't stop it. So up, up, and away I went.

I figured the son of a bitch was playing a joke on me
and sending me for a joy ride. I was going to ride down
again as soon as the cage got to the top floor so I could
have a little talk with Johnnie. But when it stopped,
there was a surprise waiting for me. My wife was
standing barefoot on the concrete apron by the elevator
gate. She was wearing a smile and nothing else.

Man, did that turn me on. I mean, here I was right in
the middle of the city on the top floor of a completely
open structure, with my wife stark naked and her
giant tits flapping in the breeze. And let me tell you
Lucy's got some big ones. She's really a hot-looking
woman, about five-seven with a tiny waist and wide
hips. Her hair is real dark, almost black, and she's got
a jungle of it down below, if you know what I mean.
Everything was showing. I just stood there gawking,
with my cock getting hard.

"Hi, big boy," she said, putting on an exaggerated
seductive voice. "Glad you could come up and see
me." She opened the elevator gate and grabbed my
hand, dragging me out of the cage. Without another
word, she unzipped my fly and pulled out my dick,
which by now was as hard as an iron bar.

Pretty as you please, she dropped to her knees on
the rough concrete and started sucking me off. When
I felt her hot mouth closing around me, all I could do
was concentrate on the sensations. Her tongue was

swabbing my tool while the skyscraper wind whistled in the girders around us. It was so sudden and unexpected that I came right away. Lucy kept on sucking me while I pumped and pumped and pumped. My eyes were shut tight, and for an instant I forgot where I was.

Just as I finished coming, Lucy started pushing me backward with her hands. When I opened my eyes, I found myself back in the cage. She slammed shut the gate, punched the button for the ground floor, and sent me on my way again. "Nothing like going down," she called as the cage descended.

When I got to the bottom, Johnnie was laughing. She had set up the whole thing with him in advance. "Hey, boss man," Johnnie teased. "Better zip up your fly."

After that, Lucy and I started to compete with each other to see who could come up with the best erotic surprise. The great thing about that kind of contest is we both are winners. We always try to outdo each other at our little sex game, but I've got to take credit for the best one of all. It was when I thought up the idea of surprising her with dessert. It was just a couple of months ago, in fact.

In the morning, we agreed to meet after work for a fancy dinner in one of our favorite restaurants. I had been hatching my scheme for a week or two. As soon as Lucy left to go to her job, I got everything ready.

That night, we had a couple of drinks and a great dinner. At the end of the meal, the waiter offered to bring coffee and a dessert tray. Lucy was about to order when I interrupted. "I don't think so," I said, winking at my wife. "Tonight we're having dessert at home." I could tell from Lucy's expression that she got my meaning. She knew a surprise was coming.

We practically fell over each other in haste as I paid the bill. Heading home, I don't know which of us was more eager for the rest of the night to unfold. As soon as we got into the house, I told Lucy to go into the bedroom, get completely undressed, and wait for me on the bed. I went to the kitchen to get the tray that I had prepared earlier and carried it into the bedroom.

Lucy had followed my instructions and was lying nude on her back on the shower curtain that I had used to cover the bed. Her legs were spread slightly to give me a view of her pussy. She knows how hot that gets me.

"What's with the plastic sheet?" she asked. Then she sat up to look curiously at the tablecloth I had thrown over the tray. "And what are you hiding under that?"

"Never mind," I answered. "Just close your eyes and leave everything to me." I could tell by the way her nipples got hard that she was excited. She lay back down, closing her eyes submissively.

Taking a jar of honey from the tray, I went to the foot of the bed. I stroked her feet with my hands and then poured some honey onto them. "What are you doing?" she asked, as the thick liquid trickled over and between her toes.

I answered without words, lifting her foot to my mouth and closing my lips around her big toe. She sighed softly when I began sucking one toe at a time, dipping my tongue into the spaces between them to lap up every drop of honey. I did the same to her other foot, her body writhing in response to the explorations of my mouth.

After I licked all the honey from her feet, I held the jar over her and drizzled long streaks of it up the entire length of her legs, watching it ooze over the insides of her thighs and drip onto the plastic sheet that covered the bed. I also poured a gob of the sticky stuff into the crater of her navel. I could see by the way her pelvis began thrusting that contact with the thick liquid was arousing her. I was in no hurry.

Slowly, with light flicks of my tongue, I began licking the honey off her skin. I started at her right ankle and trailed my way up a millimeter at a time, my mouth coming closer and closer to her pussy. The fragrance of her sexual excitement mingled with the sweet scent of honey, creating the most exotic perfume I ever inhaled. I brought my tongue to the edge of her opening and then teased her by changing direction and licking downward, concentrating on the inside of her thigh.

She began to moan as I repeated the performance on her other leg, again bringing my mouth to the brink of her sex before heading down toward her ankle. Her hairy mound was rotating in small circles as her excitement built. I placed my hand on the triangle of fur and pressed gently, feeling the moisture of desire oozing between her sex lips.

Bending over her, I licked around the outside of her navel, enjoying the sweet flavor of the honey mixed with the salty taste of her excited perspiration. I dipped the tip of my tongue into the golden pool that the nectar formed in the pit of her belly button. She lifted her ass off the mattress, trying to press herself harder against my face, but I pulled back slightly to keep the contact light and teasing.

Lucy has a sensitive navel and always likes it when I lick her there in our foreplay. The sticky substance must have increased her sensitivity, because as I lapped at it with hungry strokes of my tongue, her moans got louder. I kept it up until I had swallowed every drop. By now she was beside herself, her body moving violently on the bed.

Dipping two of my fingers into the honey jar, I rubbed it softly onto the open lips of her pussy. She practically howled at the touch. I returned to the jar for more, and then did it again, until every bit of pink membrane was shining with the syrupy coating. Pouring generously from the jar, I drenched her clit, watching it swim in the amber fluid.

Lucy convulsed with excitement, her hips thrashing from side to side. Her legs spread apart even farther, her sexual opening begging for more attention. The honey on her pussy seemed to be bubbling with her heat. I began rubbing it, inserting my fingers between the lips to carry some of the sweetness inside. With the tips of my index and middle fingers, I traced a circle around the throbbing button of her clit, bringing her almost to the edge of climax. When I stopped, she groaned a plea for satisfaction.

In response, I licked lightly at her sex lips. The honey sweetened the spicy female flavor, exciting me almost as much as it was exciting her. I delved deep with the blade of my tongue, plunging it inside to extract the combination of sweet syrup and lovejuice. The sounds she made inspired me to perform intricate maneuvers with my lips and mouth. I turned her pussy inside out to suck hungrily at it. I lapped around its edges, bringing soft cries of desire from her throat. Finally, I closed my mouth around her clit.

She practically hit the ceiling. I sucked and I licked, lapping at the sticky syrup that coated her most sensitive spot. The taste was changing, sweetness giving way to the tart erotic savor of her preorgasmic secretions. I sucked harder, pressing my mouth tight against her mound to form with my lips a protective circle around her clit. I made a buzzing sound in the back of my throat, which set my whole mouth vibrating to increase her pleasure.

With a cry, she reached a climax. Her juices poured from her opening, coating the honeyed walls of her vagina and wetting the insides of her thighs. I licked her until she placed her hands on my head and pushed me away. She lay there panting, trying to calm herself after her explosive orgasm.

Before she could completely recuperate, I brought on the second course. Her eyes were open now. She seemed to watch helplessly as I poured warm fudge sauce over and around her breasts. The gooey syrup coated the crinkled red nubbins of her nipples and circled the pebbly disks surrounding them. When the smooth skin of her big round tits was crisscrossed with dark-chocolate lines, I sprinkled them with flakes of white candy.

Shaking a can of whipped cream, I sprayed a snowy cap onto each of her mountains. I decorated each swelling breast with banana slices and a bright red cherry from a bowl on the tray. I took a plump strawberry and used it to dab some of the fudge sauce from her breast. After dipping it into the whipped cream, I offered it to her, holding the sweetened berry to her lips.

After she ate it, I helped myself to one. First I stroked her softly with it, coating the red fruit with syrup. Then I trailed the chocolate-covered strawberry around both nipples, picking up some of the whipped cream and candy flakes. Scooping a banana slice onto the erotic confection, I bit into it, exposing the fleshy inside of the strawberry. I rubbed its juicy surface against her nipple, burrowing through the dollop of whipped cream toward its peak before popping the rest of the berry into my mouth.

Lucy was becoming aroused again by our erotic feast. When I started licking the coatings directly from her skin, she moaned. I used my tongue like a paintbrush, dabbing in little strokes that stimulated her to make rhythmic movements with her hips and pelvis. I licked steadily, starting at the base of one breast and trailing my tongue all around it before sliding its tip across the valley of her cleavage to begin on the other. I took my time, coming nearer and nearer to her nipples without actually making contact with them.

When I finally had both tits licked clean, I took one nipple in my mouth and sucked on it. By now I knew she was ready to be fucked. It would culminate our erotic dessert. Holding a can of whipped cream in each hand, I garnished the entire front of her body with the fluffy white topping.

She made little sobbing sounds as the airy substance swirled and flowed over her to tickle and titillate her skin. The warmth of her body made the cream velvety and light, and sent it seeking its way into her every nook and cranny. When the cream had formed a two-inch cushion that covered her completely, I sprayed the last of it onto my pulsating erection. Lucy's eyes widened with excitement when she realized what was about to happen.

I knelt on the edge of the bed and lowered my body onto hers. The whipped cream compressed between us, our combined body heat melting it a little, making us slick with it. I moved my torso from side to side, slipping and sliding against her. The smoothness of the cream softened the roughness of my skin. I stroked her tits with my chest, feeling my own nipples harden as they made contact with hers.

My cock was moving by itself, seeking the heat of her welcoming pussy. Her hips lifted, raising her opening high to make the entry easier. When the throbbing tip found her slit, it fell inside, lubricated by the thick coating of whipped cream. At the moment of penetration we both gasped. Neither one of us was prepared for the sudden rush of ecstasy that swept over us. I plunged forward, burying the entire length of my hard-on within her.

We began thrusting together in rhythm. Each instroke brought me right to the center of her sex, making my scrotum swing forward to slap gently against her cream-coated ass. When I drew back, the cream glued us together for a moment, connecting our writhing bodies. We continued to slide against each other as we fucked. Lucy wrapped her legs around my waist to keep me from slipping away and to pull me tight against her, my cock driving once more to her center.

"Oh, Carl," she whimpered. "You fuck me so good. Oh, Carl. I'm going to come. Again."

I felt it too, that wonderful friction beginning in my balls and forcing its way up through my cock. With each plundering thrust, the internal tingling increased. It was becoming almost unbearable. We drove harder and deeper, each stroke bringing us closer to a shared orgasm.

It hit like a blast of dynamite. I pumped my come into her while she poured her juices over my cock. The spasms of pleasure had me shuddering and gyrating, oblivious to the world around me. I heard nothing but Lucy's guttural cries as she rose to sexual satisfaction.

We clawed at each other, frantic to extinguish the fires consuming us. We came forever, riding to the heights before drifting slowly back down to earth. When it was over, we were totally exhausted and totally content.

Shit, man. That was something.

I hope I didn't shock you with my story or the language I used. You asked me about the best sex I ever had. So I told it like it was.

7

MORE THAN
TWO

Although very few have actually experienced it, many people are stimulated by the thought of group sex. Knowing this, authors of pornographic novels and producers of X-rated films routinely fill their work with scenes involving more than two people. Obviously, the idea is not new. Similar depictions appeared on Greek vases in the fifth century B.C. and on the walls of ancient Indian temples.

Group sex generally comes in two varieties. In one form, two or more couples make love in the same room, each stimulated by the presence of the other. They may exchange mates, but each person has only one partner at a time. In the other form, one or more members of the group has several partners simultaneously.

According to some sources, orgies and "swing parties" were commonplace during the 1970s in every suburban community in the United States. Psychologists and sociologists doubt that this was so. Whatever the actual frequency of group sex in our society, its popular presence in erotic art and entertainment proves that it is on the minds of many people.

In gathering material for *Whispered Secrets*,[1] our book about sexual fantasy, we found group-sex fantasies to be among the most common described by the people we interviewed. However, we also found that as a real-life practice, it is rather unusual. While it may be pleasant to imagine the simultaneous touch of many hands or the taste of many bodies, group sex is not for everyone. Insecurity is often generated by the troubling question: "Is my partner enjoying that other person's touch more than mine?" The jealousy that results from observing a lover in the arms of another can seriously jeopardize a relationship.

The people who told us the stories that follow claim that their experiments caused no damage and, in fact, led to the best sex they ever had. If this is so, they belong to a relatively small and rare breed of human. Even for them, however, these activities are what one described as "the kind of thing you do maybe once in a lifetime."

*Iris and Steven Finz, *Whispered Secrets: The Couple's Guide to Erotic Fantasy*. New York: Signet, 1990.

MIXED DOUBLES

At thirty-six, Sid appears ten *years younger. His small wiry body is agile and firm. His brown eyes are clear and sparkling. His hair is dark and expensively groomed. Sid, an investment broker, spends two or three days a week on the golf course, where he conducts a substantial portion of his business. His petite wife, Emily, thirty-four, is a licensed interior designer. Sid says that he and Emily had their best sex ever when they reunited with their old college flames.*

♥   ♥   ♥

Emily and I give a lot of parties. My business pretty much requires it. People let me invest millions of dollars for them. Let's face it, nobody likes to trust a stranger with that kind of money. So I've always thought it a good practice to make my clients think of me not just as a broker but as a friend, too.

When we bought our house, we looked for a place that would be right for entertaining. The dining room seats thirty or forty people comfortably, and in warm weather, our parties usually spill over onto the patio. We're on top of a hill, with no neighbors in the immediate vicinity, so we never have to worry about noise and we can have live bands whenever we choose to.

On this particular night, there were about twenty couples, all laughing and drinking and dancing and having a good time. Emily and I were taking turns answering the door to welcome latecomers. It was my turn when the Baxters arrived. There was another couple with them.

"I hope you don't mind," Jim Baxter said, shaking my hand and moving off to one side. "Bruce and Lois dropped in on us as we were getting ready to leave for your party. When we told them where we were going, they insisted on coming along. Bruce says that you all knew each other back in college."

"That's right," I answered, shaking hands with Bruce and kissing Lois on the cheek. "We haven't seen each other in years. Thanks for bringing them, Jim."

I really was glad to see them. Actually, we were more than old college buddies. Although Bruce had majored in psychology while I was working toward my MBA, we both belonged to the same fraternity and saw quite a bit of each other. But there was more to it than that.

Bruce and my wife, Emily, had dated for almost two years and were practically engaged at one point. Emily told me that the engagement was the reason their relationship ended. Dating had been fine, but when they got serious about marriage, she realized that Bruce was not the person she wanted to spend the rest of her life with.

Lois and I, on the other hand, had never gotten serious about anything, although we had lived together for about nine months. Neither of us had ever really expected our relationship to last. It was never more than one of those college things that seemed right at the time. That had been good enough for us.

Lois and I had broken up on good terms. Soon afterward, she started going out with Bruce. After college we sort of drifted apart. Then, a year or so later, I heard that Bruce and Lois got married.

I had first met Emily when she was engaged to Bruce, but we didn't really get to know each other until about four years ago. It was quite a coincidence. I called an agency to have my apartment redecorated, and Emily was the decorator they sent. We recognized each other right away and started talking about all the people we used to know.

Well, there just wasn't time in the workday for all the catching up we had to do, so I asked her to have dinner with me. We hit it off immediately, and I guess you could say we've been having dinner together ever since. We were married just a few months later.

After greeting Bruce and Lois, I led them through the crowd in search of Emily. She was surprised and glad to see them. We were so busy with our other guests during the course of the evening, though, that neither of us had much time to spend with our old friends. Later, as the crowd began to thin, Emily suggested that Bruce and Lois stay after everyone else was gone so that we could all get reacquainted.

We sat on the patio together, sharing several bottles of wine and bringing one another up to date. They were living on the East Coast and had come to town for Bruce to attend a conference. He was a psychologist with a successful practice and had written several pop-psych books that placed him somewhat in demand as a speaker. His age was showing a bit, but Lois looked young and ravishing. While her husband cured the neuroses of society, she spent her time tanning, swimming, and exercising her trim body.

As I looked at her, I found myself remembering the old days when we would lie in bed together making love for hours at a time. I guess I was undressing her in my head as the four of us chatted and got tipsy.

When Emily suggested that we all soak in the Jacuzzi, it sounded like a great idea to me.

Lois asked if she could borrow a bathing suit. "What for?" I said. "We're all grown-ups, and none of us will be seeing anything we haven't seen before. So why bother with suits?"

I don't know what would have happened if we hadn't all consumed as much wine as we did, but as it was, everybody found my suggestion appealing. Within minutes, we were all nude and climbing into the bubbling spa. Bruce stared openly at my wife, appraising her naked body without pretense.

"Emily," he said, sitting on the concrete bench in the spa. "You look terrific. You really haven't changed a bit." Emily smiled and sort of pranced in the churning water. "Except," he added thoughtfully, "I think your tits might be sagging a little."

Emily looked challenged. "What?" she sputtered. "My tits don't sag at all. They're just as firm as they ever were." Stepping up in front of where Bruce was sitting, she pushed her shoulders back to thrust her breasts forward. "Here," she said. "Feel for yourself."

Before I had a chance to react, Bruce boldly cupped my wife's breasts in his hands, squeezing gently as if to measure their heft. I could see her pink nipples hardening. Without letting go, he said, "No, you're right. These tits are every bit as firm as the last time I held them." I didn't exactly know why, but I felt my cock stirring.

Still holding Emily's boobs, Bruce said, "Most psychologists believe that there is no jealousy in true love." Turning suddenly to me, he asked, "Well, Sid. Is your love for Emily true? Or is it making you jealous to see me fondling her tits?" A worried look passed across Emily's face, but she just stood there allowing him to handle her.

"Not at all," I answered. "In fact, I'm finding it rather exciting." I looked at Emily and saw her smile with relief. "But do you practice what you preach?" I asked. "What if I felt Lois's ass? Would that bother you?"

As I spoke, I moved in front of where Lois was standing and looked her in the eye. Her expression gave me permission. Reaching around her, I took her buttocks in my hands and stroked them gently. My cock became rock hard instantly as I caressed my former girlfriend while her husband and my wife looked on.

"It doesn't bother me at all," Bruce answered. I could see that he also had a hard-on. "After all, you probably screwed her a thousand times before she started going out with me. What difference would it make if you did it again now?"

At his words, Lois reached down and grabbed my cock. "I'd love it," she said. "I'd love to fuck you again. For old times' sake. That is, if it would be all right with Emily."

I knew my wife well enough to recognize the look of desire passing across her face. It was obvious that she was enjoying the touch of Bruce's fingers, which had now moved to her nipples where they were tracing little circles. It was also obvious that she was intrigued by the idea of watching me and Lois get it on.

I realized that if I did it with Lois, I would, in effect, be giving my wife permission to do it with Bruce. But I did not find the thought at all distasteful. What Bruce said made a lot of sense to me. They did plenty of fucking when they were engaged. I always knew that, of course, and it never was a problem for me. In fact, occasionally I used to imagine the two of them together, and the image always turned me on.

I like to think of myself as open-minded where sex is concerned. I don't have a problem with jealousy, and as far as I know, neither does Emily. What we know about each other's past relationships never interferes with Emily's feelings for me or with my feelings for her. Why should it matter if she and her former lover had sex again now? Actually, the thought of watching Emily with Bruce while I did it with Lois was very exciting.

It must have had the same effect on Emily. Her husky voice could barely be heard over the sound of the Jacuzzi as she said, "Yes. I love the idea. Let's have an orgy."

The moment the words left Emily's lips, Lois began stroking my erection up and down. Having received Emily's consent, I abandoned myself to sex with Bruce's wife. Clutching the cheeks of her ass, I pulled her against me until the tip of my dick was grazing the patch of curly hair around her pussy. "Yes," she whispered, placing her lips against my ear and running her tongue over it.

She moved her hips from side to side, rubbing her pubis against my erect penis and pressing her breasts tightly against my chest. I could feel her hard nipples boring into me like diamond-tipped drills. My fingers began searching between the round cheeks of her ass for the tight little crevasse that I knew nestled in the valley. When I found it, I nudged lightly at it. Lois always was sensitive back there and I always knew that I could whip her up to feverish passion by caressing her between the cheeks.

She was groaning with complete lack of inhibition, her eyes shut tight and her mouth wide open. Allowing the heated water to buoy her up, she wrapped her legs around mine and thrust her pelvis toward me, all the while chewing and nibbling at my ear. "Yes," she moaned. "Put your cock in me. Fuck me. Just like you used to."

Her words sent chills through my pulsating body, increasing my excitement. I humped forward, aiming my throbbing cock for her opening. When I felt it encounter the lips of her pussy, I hesitated for a moment, savoring the pleasure of anticipation. "Put it in me," she commanded, her voice becoming louder. "Put your big cock in me while Emily and Bruce watch. I want them to see it. I want them to see you fucking me."

I had to tighten all the muscles in my groin to keep from coming instantly. For a few moments, I had been lost, so absorbed in the ecstasy of sexual contact with Lois that I forgot where we were and who we were with. Her words brought me back to a reality that carried my arousal to a peak.

Looking over Lois's shoulder, I saw my wife in the embrace of her former fiancé. They were kissing, their tongues probing deep in each other's mouths. One of Bruce's arms was around Emily's waist, pulling her against him, while his other hand played with her breasts, gently pinching and rolling the nipples. Emily's hands were between their bodies. Although I couldn't see them, it was clear that she was holding and rubbing his cock beneath the bubbly water.

Emily's eyes were open, staring at Lois and me. Without making a sound, she moved her lips, mouthing at me the words, "Fuck her." I was so excited I thought I'd have a heart attack. My throbbing dick found its mark and was beginning to force its way between the resilient lips of Lois's pussy. She groaned, exaggerating a bit for dramatic effect, acutely aware of Emily's staring eyes upon us.

"Yes," Lois hissed as my cock slowly entered her. "Yes, you're in me. Oooh, you're inside me. Oooh,

Bruce, watch us. He's fucking me. Sid is fucking me."

"I know," Bruce answered, his breathing labored. "I'm watching you. I see everything. Oh, yes, Sid, do it. I'm going to do it to Emily now. May I, Emily?"

"Yes," Emily responded, almost singing the word. "Yes, Bruce, put it in me."

I was all the way inside Lois now, our bodies grinding together in the swirling water of the bubbling spa. With her legs wrapped around mine, I turned so that we could watch our spouses as we plunged in intercourse. I saw Bruce drive his hips forward and heard Emily groan. I couldn't see their genitals, but I was sure that he had penetrated my wife the way I was penetrating Lois.

The air was filled with sex. It mingled with the steamy vapors rising from the churning whirlpool to create the erotic atmosphere of a sultry swamp. The music of our moans and sobs was a symphony of desire. It was like an orgy at a public bath in ancient Rome.

I felt the membranes of Lois's pussy cling lovingly to my thrusting staff, but my pleasure far exceeded what resulted from the gentle friction. There was something so thrilling that I can't even describe in the sensation of fucking another man's wife while he and my wife watched. Seeing the two of them going at it at the same time is what really drove me to the top.

I knew exactly how it felt to be inside Emily's pussy and I could imagine what Bruce was experiencing. My wife's facial expressions told me exactly what she was doing with the muscles of her pelvis. The fascination of watching her do it to another man brought me to a new high.

Sex with Emily is totally different from sex with Lois. When I'm inside Emily, her vaginal tunnel caresses my cock continually, trailing long, soft waves of pleasure over its entire length without stopping. Lois's pussy seemed to grab at me, squeezing my dick in spurts, with little rest periods in between, each constricting throb more powerful than the last.

Fucking Lois and watching Emily with Bruce, I was able to experience both lovemaking styles simultaneously. To magnify the excitement, I realized that all of us were sharing these thoughts and sensations. Emily and Lois were probably comparing my cock to Bruce's, just as Bruce and I were comparing their vulvas.

I watched Emily's body undulate as she impaled herself rhythmically on Bruce's erection. Her legs were wrapped around his hips. I could see the muscles of his upper thighs straining as he struggled to support her weight while thrusting in and out of her. Emily's eyes were open, her gaze alternating between Bruce and us. When I saw them begin to glaze over, I knew that her orgasm was approaching.

She seemed to retreat into a private world of erotic ecstasy. I realized that each drive of Bruce's plunging hard-on brought her closer to sexual climax. For the first time I felt a pang of jealousy at the thought that any man besides me could bring her that much pleasure. Then she started making sounds that told me her orgasm was beginning, and somehow my jealousy drowned in the erotic flood.

The sights and sounds and sensations were all uniting to bring me to sexual completion. Lois was panting and sobbing in my ear, thoroughly aroused at witnessing the release of Emily's passion. It had been so long since she and I had made love that I didn't know how to read her signs. Heroically, I struggled to hold back my onslaught, to be sure that Lois was satisfied before I let go. But the surge was much too strong to be controlled. I couldn't wait any longer.

Like a rocket smashing the sound barrier, my orgasm burst forth through my feeble resistance. For a moment I lost all awareness, conscious only of the streams of fluid that I was pumping deep into Lois's hungry loins. I returned to my surroundings in time to realize that all four of us were coming together. Lois's cries blended symphonically with Emily's; my gasping breaths harmonized with the grunting intonations of Bruce's masculine voice. The heated water of the spa seemed to melt us all down into a single seething organism instead of four individual beings.

Once again, I lost consciousness of reality. I drifted off on a plane of erotic fulfillment until, without quite knowing how I got there, I found myself sitting in the bubbling water with my wife on my lap. Looking across the churning pool, I saw Lois resting in her husband's arms. We were all back where we belonged.

Later that night when Emily and I were alone, we talked about the events of the evening. Emily found the whole episode very exciting, but admitted that she too experienced some jealousy at times. We agreed that although it might have been the best sex we ever had, it was the kind of thing you do maybe once in a lifetime.

Since then we've continued to have a great life together. Sex is always beautiful for us, and neither of us ever wants to make love with anybody else. But every now and then, especially when we're having sex in the Jacuzzi, we talk about the night we got together with our old partners and had our little orgy.

LAS VEGAS OUTCALL

Harriet *and her husband, Randy, successfully operate their own business, manufacturing and selling mannequins for store window displays. Harriet, thirty-one, has soft black hair and big blue eyes. She stands five feet eight inches tall, her rounded breasts and hips giving her body the sensuous softness that inspired Randy to create their highly salable full-figured mannequins. Although Randy's hands produce the product, Harriet is the brain behind the business, in charge of marketing, advertising, selling, and everything else that needs to be done. Harriet says that they had their best sex a few months ago while celebrating an important sale that she had made to a department store chain.*

♥   ♥   ♥

Randy was so excited when I told him about the deal that he grabbed one of the mannequins and danced her around the studio. Then he started dancing with me. "Let's take a few days off," he said. "We can afford it now. Let's celebrate and go to Vegas."

We had been there once before and really enjoyed it. It seemed like the kind of place where dreams just might come true. The casinos are open twenty-four hours a day and they don't even have clocks, so you never know what time it is and the fun never has to end. The idea sounded great to me. I got on the phone and booked us a flight for that very afternoon. Four hours later we were stepping out of a cab on the Las Vegas Strip.

We settled into our hotel and decided to take a little walk before dinner. Strolling along the wide boulevard, we gazed at the glitzy lights and neon that advertised the celebrities who were appearing at clubs and lounges. The streets were filled with cars, buses, and taxis, all honking their horns and jockeying for position in the mounting traffic.

Newspaper vending machines lined the sidewalks, offering free tabloids. Actually, they were advertising brochures for adult entertainments and featured garish color pictures of women in scanty outfits and lingerie. Before we returned to the hotel, Randy managed to gather an armload of them.

In our room, we lay together on the king-size bed, leafing through the pages and giggling over the suggestive ads for "Escorts" and "Private Dancers." I soon realized that some of these were really prostitution services. The language they used left very little doubt about what they were selling. Most used the word *outcall*, indicating they would come right to your hotel room for your convenience. A few of them promised "Escorts of all shapes and sizes to satisfy your every desire." One proclaimed, "You'll be so glad you came." Another said, "We specialize in men, women, and couples."

We made dinner reservations at an elegant restaurant and took our time getting ready. After we showered and dressed, we rode the elevator down to the lobby. Like all Las Vegas hotels, this one was designed in such a way that you couldn't get anyplace without walking through the bustling gambling casino. The slot machines' lights and bells were hypnotic, making it just about impossible to get past them without placing a bet or dropping a coin into one.

We found ourselves standing in front of a gleaming chrome bandit that held out the opportunity to win a million dollars with one pull of its handle. Randy was fumbling in his pockets when a hostess in a brief red outfit offered to make change. Randy handed her a twenty and received a paper cup filled with silver dollars. A glazed look in his eye, he slipped one into the slot and gestured toward the handle. "You pull it," he said. "For luck."

I reached over and yanked hard on the lever, watching the little wheels spin to display fleeting glimpses of cherries, plums, and lemons in a window at the front of the machine. Suddenly, I heard the sound of a siren and the jangling of a bell. I looked around to see where it was coming from when Randy shouted, "We won! We won! You hit the jackpot!"

People at nearby machines formed a circle around us. One asked, "How much did you win?" I had no idea.

Randy was studying the chart at the top of the machine. "You got four lemons!" he exclaimed. "Four lemons pays a thousand bucks!"

The hostess who had given him change just a few moments before stepped out of the crowd. "That's right," she said, fitting a key into the machine to silence its bell and siren. "Congratulations. I'll take you to the cashier for your payoff." In a daze, we followed her to a window that looked like a teller's station in a bank.

As if in a dream, I stood with Randy and heard the cashier ask, "How would you like the money?"

I heard my husband say, "Hundreds, please." I saw the cashier count out ten crisp one-hundred-dollar bills, but I didn't really believe any of it was happening until I saw Randy fold the money and put it in his pocket.

"Let's go eat," he said. "I think we've finished gambling."

At the dinner table, I was so excited I could hardly swallow my salad. "You picked a good machine," I said giddily. "Maybe you ought to become a professional gambler."

"Oh, no," Randy responded. "You're the one who won. After all, you pulled the handle. You should decide what we do with the money."

"Let me think about it for a while," I said, sipping my wine. "I'm still in shock."

"Me, too," Randy said. "Let's spend it impulsively."

Suddenly, I became aware of a thought that had been bouncing around secretly inside my head ever since we looked at the tabloids in our room. "I want a private dancer," I said. "Let's spend it on one of those escorts."

Randy looked shocked. "What do you mean?" he asked, obviously puzzled.

Emboldened by our victory over the slot machine, by the fantasy atmosphere that abounds in Las Vegas, and perhaps a little by the wine I was drinking, I explained breathlessly, "I want to feel two people making love to me at the same time." Looking down at my plate, I added weakly, "I'd like one of them to be you, and the other one to be a woman."

Randy stared at me in silence, a gleam of fascination lighting his eyes. "Are you serious?" he asked.

"Yes," I said. "If you'd be willing." Then, embarrassed, I blurted, "But I wouldn't want you to touch her or her to touch you. This would just be for me."

Suddenly, I felt ashamed. "Is that perverted? Or selfish?" I inquired.

Randy grinned. "Hell, no," he answered. "I think it's the most exciting thing I've ever heard."

We finished our dinner and headed back to the hotel. As soon as we were inside the room, I started thumbing through the tabloids, looking for an ad that I remembered from before. "Let's do it right now," I said. "I'm afraid I'll lose my nerve if we wait. Let's see if we can get someone for tonight."

Spotting the words "We specialize in men, women, and couples," I exclaimed, "Here it is! This one does outcalls and it says they come in all shapes and sizes. Will you call?"

"This is your night," he said. "You call and tell them exactly what you want."

Although I was nervous, I somehow managed to dial the phone and make the arrangements, receiving a promise that a woman would be at our door within an hour. It seemed that only a moment went by, though, before we heard a knock. I stood back, my heart beating wildly, as Randy opened the door to admit an attractive blond woman in a low-cut green evening dress.

"Hi," she said, flashing a friendly smile. "I'm Loni from the escort service." Randy and I stood speechless, at a total loss for words.

Loni was confident and seemed completely at ease. Closing the door behind her, she glanced at each of us. "Did you have something special in mind?" she asked. When neither of us answered, she persisted, "Am I doing him? Her? Both? Is there anything specific you want? Don't want? Would one of you kindly fill me in?" Her musical laugh made me feel a little more comfortable.

"This was my idea," I said, "so let me explain. I want both of you to make love to me. But I don't want anything to happen between you and Randy. Oh, this is my husband, Randy, and I'm Harriet."

"No problem," Loni answered. "I understand completely. It's your money. You call the shots. But I have to collect in advance. Two hundred dollars, please." As soon as Randy handed the bills to her, she tucked them in her purse and reached back to unzip her dress. Within moments she was standing before us completely naked.

The escort service had done a good job in selecting a woman to fit the description I gave them. She was in her late twenties, about five-foot-four, with a trim waist and wide hips. Although her breasts were quite large, they did not sag, but jutted out proudly from her chest, the erect nipples pointing slightly upward. Her heart-shaped face was surrounded by blond curls, but the hair of her bush was dark brown. She had a smoothly rounded bottom. I noticed Randy studying her candidly, and for some reason I found that exciting.

She turned slowly in place so that we could both get a good clear look at her. Then she said, "Come on, you two. How about getting your clothes off so the fun can begin."

I watched Randy undo his fly and step out of his pants. His penis was already hard, sticking straight out in front of him. I didn't mind a bit when I saw Loni looking at it. Then she looked expectantly at me. Nervous once again, I began to undress, concentrating on the task so I wouldn't have to meet Loni's eyes or Randy's.

As I stripped, Loni chattered to relieve the tension. "This is your first time," she said. "I can tell. Well, don't worry about it. I get calls like this all the time. You'd be surprised how many couples want it just the way you do. All kinds of people."

By now I was nude and could feel goose bumps all over my body. "Why don't you lie back on the bed?" Loni suggested. "Let me and your husband make you feel good."

I closed my eyes as I did so, but when I felt hands moving softly over my bare belly, I had to open them. I didn't want to miss any of the sensations. I wanted to see everything that was being done to me. I wanted to memorize pictures of this experience so that I could enjoy them again later.

Randy stood beside the bed, watching as Loni's fingers trailed expertly over my naked skin. She sat beside me, facing me, with her bare hip pressed against mine. Delicately, she cupped my breasts. I felt my nipples harden as she stroked them. At first her touch was so gentle that I was barely aware of it. Gradually, though, she began kneading and twisting my nipples, sending bolts of tingling pleasure through me.

I stared at the woman's breasts, watching her nipples harden with mine. I was aching to touch them but didn't have the nerve. Leaning forward, Loni moved closer. "Go ahead," she suggested. "Hold them. It feels good. Do the same things I'm doing to you."

I looked at Randy, who was watching wide-eyed, his erection throbbing with excitement. Wordlessly, he nodded in agreement to her suggestion. Tentatively, I reached for the smooth globes of her bosom. When my hands made contact with them, a shiver of excitement passed over me. It was the first time I had ever touched any breasts but my own. The naughtiness of it was thrilling. Especially with my husband there to see it all.

I began to experiment, taking the dark nipples between my thumbs and forefingers. I could feel them become even harder in response to my caresses. Gently, I rolled them, imagining what it would be like to suck on one of them. The excitement that came from having my breasts and nipples stroked by a woman while I did the same to her made me brave. Lifting my head from the pillow, I parted my lips.

Loni recognized my desire immediately, moving to bring her nipples within inches of my mouth. "Go ahead," she whispered. "I like it."

The shock of excitement that thrashed my loins almost overpowered me as I licked lightly at one swollen rosebud. I felt my juices flow copiously, wetting the lips of my vagina as my tongue laved the crinkly skin that capped her breasts. In response to my sucking, Loni passed one of her hands slowly across the naked plane of my abdomen, seeking my trembling pubic mound.

She pressed her palm against my sex hair. The tips of her fingers began to tease at the full lips of my vulva, picking up droplets of moisture and spreading them upward toward the pulsating button of my clitoris. As she rubbed little circles around it, I felt one of her fingers slipping inside me, probing deeper, until it impaled me completely. I fell back, sighing, my mouth leaving her breast.

With a strangled groan, Randy dropped to his knees beside the bed, his lips seeking my turgid nipple. Loni cupped the fullness of my flesh, holding it up to him with her hand. When his tongue made contact with me, the combined sensations were incredible. One of her fingers was driving into my sex while her hand and his mouth worked together to bring ecstatic pleasure to my breast.

Randy began moving his head from one of my nipples to the other, sucking hungrily at them. I felt Loni's hands cup the globes of my buttocks, lifting me slightly off the mattress. Randy was blocking my view of her, but I felt the softness of her face against the skin of my inner thighs. Her hot breath washed over my sensitive tissues as she kissed softly at the tops of my legs. I could feel her lips coming closer and closer to my frantically aroused vagina, and I knew that she was going to perform cunnilingus on me.

I heard a groan of pleasure before I realized that it was coming from me. Loni's tongue snaked over my vaginal lips, darting between them for an instant to give me a preview of the excitement that was to come. She nibbled and licked at me with a gentleness and expertise that could only be found in another woman. I felt myself flowering open to receive her lingual thrusts, my loins rising to press desperately against her.

Her tongue penetrated me, parting the membranes of my sex to copulate lovingly with my vulva. Rhythmically, she drove it in and out, mimicking the movements of intercourse with indescribable tenderness. Then she withdrew it to travel upward, tracing hot little trails around the throbbing erection of my pleasure center. My clit burgeoned, jutting forth to separate the folds of flesh that protected it and to bathe in Loni's moist, hot breath.

She licked with just the right amount of pressure, not too hard, not too soft. I felt my excitement rising and feared that I would come too fast, that this delightful adventure would end as suddenly as it had begun. Sensing my anxiety, Loni drew back, placing her hand flat over my tingling vaginal plane.

"Lie on your back next to Harriet," she whispered to Randy. My husband obeyed her, reluctantly leaving my nipple to stretch out beside me on the bed. His manly erection stood straight up from the hairy jungle of his loins.

Taking my hands, Loni pulled me into position above him. She had me lie down on top of him with my back against his chest, my breasts pointing at the ceiling. I could feel his insistent penis nudging from behind at the swollen mound between my legs, trying to find its opening.

With a thrill, I felt Loni's fingers gently part the lips of my vulva, directing my rotating pelvis until the tip of his organ pressed hungrily at my slit. While she stroked the curls of my pubic hair, she spread me open to ease his penetration. At last he was inside me.

Loni stroked my breasts while Randy's penis plunged to the hilt in my wet sex. He wrapped his arms tightly around my body as he drove into me. Slowly, we moved together and apart, his erection repeatedly penetrating my inflamed interior. Just when I thought the sensations were as intense as they could possibly be, I felt Loni's tongue searching for the swollen head of my clitoris.

A sob tore involuntarily from my throat as I thrilled to the feeling of being filled by Randy's thick organ while Loni's mouth expertly titillated my most sensitive spot. I never knew that anything could be this exciting. It was like experiencing sex for the very first time. I became lost in swirling excitement, controlled completely by the ecstasy of total eroticism. I felt like I was turning inside out.

Randy's hands cupped my breasts, squeezing their softness and stroking lovingly over the nipples to bring them to maximum erection. Each movement of his fingers sent a jolt of electric energy shooting straight to my sexual center. I entered a world filled with sensuous pleasures that I had never experienced before, that I never even knew existed.

This time, when I felt my orgasm building, I wanted it to come. I wanted to feel the ultimate pleasure of intercourse with my husband while a woman's gentle tongue lapped at my clitoris, and while hands—I no longer knew whose—petted the erectness of my nipples. I was getting all the stimulation I could possibly receive. It drove me over the edge.

"Oh, God, I'm coming," I screamed, as surge after rollicking surge gushed through my body. Loni kept licking, her talented tongue taking me through an orgasm that lifted me higher than I ever knew I could fly.

"I'm going to come in you, Harriet," Randy croaked. I could feel his body tightening beneath mine, his organ swelling in preparation for emission.

"Yes," I cried. "Come in me." With that, I felt his penis begin to spurt, filling me with the fluids of his ecstasy. He groaned rhythmically, the tempo of his gasps matching the beating of our orgasmic contractions.

As my juices mingled with Randy's, Loni kept tonguing my clit to extend the climax until it seemed endless. Finally, when the pleasure was so intense that it bordered on discomfort, I felt the spasms winding down. Randy's penis softened and slipped out of me. Loni's lingual caresses lightened until I barely felt the lips of her mouth nibbling at the lips of my vagina. With a sigh, I rolled off Randy, sinking into the mattress beside him, oblivious to all sense of reality, lost in post-passion serenity.

As I came slowly to my senses, I was vaguely aware of Loni moving about the room, getting back into her clothes. When she was dressed, she smiled and said, "I hope you two have a wonderful time in Las Vegas." Without another word, she was gone, closing the door softly behind her.

For a long time, Randy and I lay together in silence. Then I told him how much I enjoyed the adventure. I tried to describe how wonderful it felt to have every part of me touched at once, all my erogenous centers stimulated simultaneously. Randy understood. I never could have experienced those sensations with Randy alone. I was grateful that he was tolerant enough to make it possible. By understanding my desires and indulging them that night, he gave me the best sex I ever had.

8

SEEING
AND BEING SEEN

No race of creatures can exist unless it is endowed with a desire for reproduction. In order to strengthen this desire in humans, Nature decorated our reproductive organs with tufts of curling hair and splashes of dramatic color to make them particularly interesting. In addition, our brains were wired with circuits that excite us upon seeing another's naked body or knowing that another is looking at ours.

Humans are not the only animals on Earth that have been blessed in these ways. Baboons wear bright colors to call attention to their genitals. Female goats who want sex wave their tails repeatedly so that the sight of their distended pudenda will attract males. When animals see other animals having intercourse, they may become so aroused that they are driven to a frenzy of violent sexual activity themselves.

Prohibitions against public sex are common in human societies. Some analysts claim that these rules exist because of fears that such displays will excite bystanders to the point of uncontrollable eroticism. In addition to disrupting the social order, there is the danger that this will interfere with productivity and promote physical aggression.

As a result, we are trained, from the time of our births, to believe that sex should happen only behind closed doors and shuttered windows. We learn to call our sex organs "private parts" and to regard people who display them as perverts or even criminals. We have laws that prohibit the exposure of the breasts and regulate the size and shape of bikinis worn on public beaches.

Most people can live comfortably with these rules. For some, however, the desire to see and be seen is a powerful erotic stimulant. When faced with the opportunity to observe others engaging in sex, they seize it without hesitation. When given the occasion to exhibit their own sexuality, they jump at the chance. These experiences are so unusual that those who have known them frequently declare that they were the best sex they ever had.

EXHIBITIONISTS

Marla is five feet four inches
tall with long, thick red hair. The freckles covering her face
and throat make her look younger than her twenty-six years.
Marla teaches yoga at a community college. Her passion for
yoga has made her body lithe and supple with a narrow waist
that flares out to wide, sensuous hips. She has been living
with her boyfriend, Dan, a computer systems analyst, for
the past eight months. Marla says her most erotic experience
occurred one night when she and Dan were visiting friends.
Her saucer-shaped brown eyes flash with suppressed merri-
ment as she describes it to us.

♥　　♥　　♥

Dan and Tony have been
friends for years. Ever since Dan and I started
dating, we've spent lots of time with Tony and
his girlfriend, Celeste. They're fun people, and we
always laugh a lot when we're together. Tony's an
accountant, and I guess I always expected accoun-
tants to be dull. But Tony isn't. Of course, he's
not just an ordinary accountant. He works for a
movie company, and maybe that makes his job
kind of glamorous. He usually has all the inside
gossip about what's going on in Hollywood. You
know, who's sleeping with who, that sort of thing.

Celeste is terrific, too. Spontaneous and impulsive. Anything to have a good time. She's never afraid of trying something new. She works as a legal secretary for a big downtown law firm. The two of us hit it off right from the beginning.

Anyway, one evening a few months ago, Tony called to invite us over for drinks. We really felt like staying home. Actually, we were planning to go to bed early for some hot sex. Dan didn't say that to Tony, of course. He just said we were kind of tired.

But Tony insisted. He said that he had something for us to see, and it had to be that night. He absolutely wouldn't take no for an answer. He said he was already popping the cork out of the wine bottle and would be expecting us within a half hour. Before Dan could make any more excuses, Tony just hung up.

We always dress casual when we go to Tony and Celeste's, so we just combed our hair and went as we were. Dan was wearing sweats—a kind of jogging suit, really. I had on jeans and a Western-style shirt with snaps down the front.

When we got to Tony's apartment, Celeste greeted us with hugs. "Come on in," she invited. "The wine is waiting."

The four of us sat on the sectional sofa around the cocktail table in the living room, chatting and sipping red wine. After a while, Dan said, "So what's the big surprise? And why did it have to be tonight?"

A mischievous smile played over Tony's face. "Wait till you see what I've got," he said. "You won't be sorry you came. You think you were fooling me with that bullshit about going to bed early because you were tired? You were going to bed early, all right, but not because you were tired. Screwing! That's what you had in mind. Don't try to kid me. But, believe me, you're going to be glad you stayed up for this."

I was dying of curiosity. "What is it?" I asked eagerly. "What is this all about?"

Tony went into the bedroom for a moment and returned with a videotape in his hand. "I've got a piece of film here with two of America's biggest movie stars in some of the hottest sex scenes ever recorded. Some of these scenes were so explicit that they had to be taken out of the film to keep it from getting an X rating. Others are just plain bloopers. It's a shame, but after tomorrow nobody's ever going to get to see them. All copies are to be destroyed at nine A.M. in the editing room. I've got a friend who smuggled this one out for me, but he made me promise that I wouldn't make copies and that I'd never tell anyone I'd seen it. I've got to return it to him first thing in the morning."

I was intrigued. When Tony dimmed the lights and popped the tape in his VCR, I stared at the TV screen. Some numbers flashed across the screen to identify the scene and take. And then it began. I wish I could tell you who the two movie stars were, but Tony made us promise that we never would. He said that if anyone found out he had shown us this film, he and his friend would both lose their jobs and would probably never work in the industry again.

I can say this, though. The male star is someone that you've probably seen in at least ten movies. And if you haven't fantasized about being kissed by him, you're just not a normal red-blooded woman. The female hasn't been around quite as long, but you'd recognize her name if you heard it. She's one of the up-and-coming young starlets, and everyone is predicting that she'll be the sex goddess of the nineties. Some say she's the new Marilyn Monroe.

When the scene opened, the two stars were in bed embracing. Although they were naked, all you could really see was their bare asses. I wondered why this scene had to be removed. I had seen plenty of movies that showed more than that. Then they broke the embrace, and I understood. When he rolled over, his mammoth erection was standing straight up in the air.

A voice in the background shouted, "Cut!" but the action continued.

This particular actor is known as a macho man, and he sure had the dick to prove it. It was thick and long and looked as hard as a tree trunk. I couldn't help staring at it. I mean, I've probably imagined that thing every time I've seen him on the screen. He's so sexy you can't help it. And here he was lying back and showing it to the world. I felt myself becoming excited immediately.

The actress didn't react that way, though. She started to laugh explosively, her hands flying up to cover her mouth. You could tell she had totally lost it. She kept laughing, her body flopping hopelessly about on the bed. She was laughing so convulsively that at one point she threw her legs out in both directions, totally exposing her pussy. I could see Dan's attention focusing on the screen. I couldn't blame him, of course. It was so exciting to see those movie stars all naked that way.

"You can't show a stiff dick in the movies," the starlet sputtered between choking laughs. The male star was laughing too, but that didn't do anything to reduce the size of his hard-on. "You'll get the whole production company arrested," she said.

"What the hell am I supposed to do about it?" he said, roaring with uninhibited laughter. "I'm in bed with the sexiest woman in Hollywood. Don't blame me, blame him." He pointed dramatically at his penis, absolving himself of all responsibility.

"Well, we'll have to do something," she said, her body shaking with amusement. "Here, I'll take care of it. Then we can get on with making this film." With that, she grabbed his penis in her hand and began jerking it vigorously up and down, still laughing. Her actions were making his laughter subside until it became more like a moan. A voice kept shouting "Cut! Cut!" But no one was cutting anything.

The actress continued rubbing his dick, her movements no longer quite as rough. Her rhythm was slower and more in tune to the involuntary gyrations of his hips. He wasn't laughing at all now. His eyes were closed and his body was rocking.

The sight of my film idol getting a handjob was really affecting me. I could feel myself becoming wet in the pants. It must have been arousing Dan too, because he moved over closer to me and put his arm around my shoulders.

The big cock on the screen seemed to be growing even bigger, swelling and turning beet red as the stroking became more loving than playful. I was sure that the screen would go black at any minute, but it didn't. I was glad. I wanted to see more. There's something exciting about seeing other people make love. And when they're movie stars, it's major erotic.

I tried to imagine what it was like for the actress to be jerking off that gorgeous hunk. Judging from the expression on her face, she was enjoying it. She was obviously the kind of woman who really got into sex. She was staring at the throbbing erection with the same fascination that I was. As we both watched it, it seemed to rear back, getting ready to buck.

The camera zoomed in on the bulbous head just as the first whirling white drop of semen shot out of it. The thick liquid flew from the tip of that movie star's dick with the power of a shot fired from a cannon.

Then it was followed by another. And another. I think that watching a man come is about the most intimate thing you can do. But watching this particular man come was almost too exciting for me to bear.

I heard the sound of heavy breathing and realized it was my own. Dan must have heard it too, because he pulled me toward him and patted my breast with his hand, whispering seductively, "Pretty hot, isn't it?" I felt my nipples growing rock hard against the inside of my bra.

To my disappointment, the screen faded to black. Almost immediately, numbers flashed again. "This is the next take of that same scene," Tony said. "That handjob cost the studio a few thousand bucks. They had to wait an hour before the star was ready to work again, while everybody on the set continued to get paid."

"How many people were on the set?" my curiosity prompted me to ask. The idea intrigued me.

Tony, with his accountant's brain, knew exactly. "With the cameramen, the production staff, and the gofers," he said, "there were seventeen. Not counting the actors."

"Seventeen," I echoed. "God, it must have been exciting for the actors to be doing that in front of seventeen people. I can just imagine."

"Exciting?" Celeste said. "I would be too embarrassed to get excited. But I'll bet it was thrilling to be one of the people watching. Now that's something I could really get excited about."

On the screen, the second take of the scene began the way it had the first time, with the actor and actress on the bed tightly embracing in the nude. They kissed for a while, and then he slipped his hand between their bodies to fondle one of her breasts. She moved back slightly so that we could see the rounded fullness of her. Her nipple was cherry red and hard. This may have been only a scene in a movie, but that nipple erection was no act. His head dipped to stroke her breasts with his cheek before he took the erect nipple in his mouth.

I felt Dan's thigh pressing mine as he pulled me tight against him. He began stroking my breasts through my shirt with both his hands. I watched the lovers on the screen while I let Dan feel me up. It was so exciting. When I felt the top two snaps of my shirt pop open, I purred. As Dan slipped a hand inside, I felt another snap open. Grabbing the front of my shirt, I pulled sharply, opening the rest of the snaps in a single stroke.

The movie star's mouth was moving from one erect nipple to the other as Dan stroked me through the satin fabric of my bra. I ached for my breasts to be free. I wanted to feel his breath on them. I wanted his tongue to touch and tease them. I wanted to feel what the actress was feeling. With swift fingers, I undid the fastener at the front of my bra and shrugged it open. Dan cupped my breasts in his hands and squeezed them softly. For the moment, we had both forgotten that we were not alone.

"Oh, Dan," I moaned as his fingers played with my exposed breasts. "Oh, yes. That feels so good."

Tony's voice brought me back. "Hey, you guys," he said. "What are you going to do, fuck right here?"

I felt a tingling in my pussy. Tony might have been kidding, but his suggestion excited me. Dan started to pull away from my tits, but I covered his hands with mine and held them in place. "That's a hot idea," I said softly, looking to Tony and Celeste for a response.

Celeste's breathing was deep and labored, her bosom rising and falling with each inhale and exhale. "I think it's a hot idea, too," she said in a voice that trembled with excitement. "Why don't you go for it, Marla?"

"Well, I certainly have no objection," Tony added, his voice sounding nervously eager.

"Now it's up to Dan," I said, freeing his hands and leaning back to give him full access to my breasts. My boyfriend hesitated for a split second and then, without a word, fell forward, taking one of my nipples in his mouth and sucking gently on it.

The couple on the screen were fucking now, but we were too involved in our own activity to give them any more attention. As Dan licked my breasts, his hands worked my shirt and bra off over my shoulders and arms. It was exciting to be exposed in front of our friends' watching eyes. Dan cupped my breasts with his hands as I helped him out of his jogging suit.

When he was naked, he stood up, his hard cock pointing straight out in front of him. Then he drew me to my feet and started unbuttoning my jeans. I had a sense of unreality. I couldn't believe it was happening. He slid the jeans down to where I could step out of them, leaving me clad only in my white cotton panties.

Taking my hand, Dan turned me in a complete circle, so that Tony and Celeste could see every part of me. I could feel their eyes burning my skin, arousing me more than I had ever been aroused before. I was acutely conscious of the triangle of red hair that almost showed through the thin fabric of my panties. I wanted to be completely naked. I wanted nothing hidden.

Without waiting for Dan's next move, I stripped the panties off and tossed them out of the way. I stroked my curling bush and pressed the palm of one hand against my moist slit. "Come on, Dan," I whispered hoarsely. "I want you to do me while Tony and Celeste watch." I moved to the couch and lay back on it, slowly parting my legs so that they could look between them. The idea of being on display for the hungry, lustful gaze of our best friends had my juices flowing incredibly.

Dan moved slowly toward me, his erection bobbing up and down with each step. His cock was beautiful, but all the eyes in the room, even Celeste's, were on me. Dan sat on the couch beside me and stared into my slit. Softly, he touched its lips with the fingers of both hands, spreading them to turn my pussy into a blossoming flower. I could feel the stares as his fingertips stroked and petted the moist folds of flesh. I closed my eyes in pleasure and then forced them open again so that I could see the people who were watching me.

Celeste had the glazed look of someone in a hypnotic trance. Tony was leaning forward in his seat so that he wouldn't miss a thing. When Dan slipped one thick finger inside my pussy, I heard Celeste sigh quietly. A moment later, she was sitting on Tony's lap and kissing him, while her eyes remained open and fastened on me.

Dan stroked his finger in and out of me until it was gleaming with the wetness of my sex. My hips moved rhythmically up and down, matching the tempo of his movement. I could hear the slurping noises made by my juices as his finger whipped them to a froth. When I remembered that our friends could hear the same sounds, I got even wetter. Dan slipped a second finger in now, stretching me open wider as if to prepare me for the onslaught of his cock.

I kissed Dan's ear, bathing it with the tip of my tongue, and whispered in a voice loud enough for Celeste and Tony to hear, "I think they like it. Why don't you fuck me now and really give them something to look at?"

With his hands, Dan guided me from the couch to the floor. He stood over me, his feet apart and his back to the watchful couple on the couch. Gracefully, he lowered himself to his knees, shuffling forward an inch at a time until I could feel the heat of his body radiating against my skin. I placed the backs of my ankles on his shoulders as he hunched forward. The tip of his swollen penis was nudging at me now. I wanted to throw myself upward to swallow it in a single thrust, but I knew it would be best if I left everything to Dan's superb sense of timing. He can stretch out the actual penetration so long that it seems to go on forever.

I wanted to scream with hungry desperation. Then I felt the head of his penis spreading my labia as he buried his massive hard-on inside me by slow and steady degrees. I groaned, conscious somewhere in the bottom of my being that our audience was waiting, breathless, for him to drive it into me to the hilt.

I always liked fucking in this position because it made possible the deepest kind of penetration. I groaned again as I felt the mass of him strike against my cervix. Arching my back, I lifted my sex up to him, silently begging for the last inch of his cock. With a bestial grunt, he rammed forward, giving me his all.

I sobbed with emotion as he began fucking in and out of me as hard as he could with long driving strokes. His forward thrust dragged a groan from my throat, followed an instant later by the groans of Celeste and Tony. Knowing that they were watching us have sex on their living room floor increased my excitement. I never realized before what an exhibitionist I was, or how thrilling it could be to be the center of everyone's erotic attention. My entire body was bathed in sweat.

I groaned. I sighed. I moaned. I went wild. I was like a wild animal, humping vigorously to match the violence of his thrusts. Our excitement was so intense that I knew neither of us would be able to keep this up for very long. Never before had I experienced a passion of such power. I could feel my climax building. I knew Dan well enough to know that his, too, was just an instant away.

"Oh, Dan," I wailed. "I'm going to come. Oh, Tony. Oh, Celeste. Watch me. Watch me. Watch me." That was it; the waiting time was over. Like a dam bursting, my climax overtook me, drowning all thought, flushing away all contact with reality. For a few moments, I was lost.

Dan's voice brought me back. "I'm coming, too," he groaned. His ass bucked ferociously as he pumped his semen deep into my tunnel. I felt his hard-on throbbing inside me and I was suddenly aware again of our audience. I moaned for them as much as for myself. Dan and I kept rolling together until our energy ran out. I lowered my legs. With a sigh, Dan slumped forward to come to rest on top of me.

We lay that way for a while, Dan with his eyes closed while I watched Tony and Celeste kissing deeply. The TV screen had gone dark. Tony broke the kiss and glanced at us, as if to assure himself that our performance had really ended. He rose to his feet, lifting Celeste into his arms, and said, "We're going to the privacy of our own bedroom now. But when we close our eyes, you can be sure we'll be seeing you." Carrying his girlfriend out of the room, he was gone.

Dan and I dressed hurriedly, eager to rush home to make love again. Which we did. Putting on that erotic performance for Tony and Celeste had whipped us up to a pitch of excitement that didn't subside for weeks. In a way, it never subsided. Dan and I have fantastic sex almost every night. But without a doubt, the best sex we ever had was the night we did it for an audience.

CAMPING OUT

Neal played football when he was in college and still looks it even though he is now thirty-two years old. His rippling muscles and flat abdomen make it obvious that he works at staying in good shape. His straw-colored hair has a way of falling in front of his light brown eyes that makes him appear boyish and uncertain. As a lawyer, however, he is known to be a tough adversary. His wife, Karen, a high school principal, is thirty-three. Neal says the best sex he ever had was on a camping trip he and Karen took on an impulse one weekend.

♥　♥　♥

I was a pretty good football player in college. And Karen was a cheerleader. She was really something. I guess we both lost interest in sports after college. I stayed in shape, but Karen has gotten a little chunky over the years. Not that it bothers me. I think flesh is sexy.

Anyway, this incident happened last year during the World Series. Those games were all anybody around here could talk about. Our friends, our neighbors, my law partners, everyone had baseball fever. Everyone but us, that is.

THE BEST SEX I EVER HAD

I'm not sure whether it was Karen or me, but one of us got the idea that with everybody else home watching what could be the last game of the Series, it would be a great weekend for taking a trip. We decided to go camping—something we do infrequently enough for it to still be an enjoyable novelty. I borrowed a tent from one of my partners, threw the sleeping bags in the trunk of the car, and we headed out of town. We were planning to get in a bit of weekend screwing and were both excited about the idea of sex in a tent.

We drove for about two-and-a-half hours. As we traveled, we whiled away the time making sex talk. Karen said that she wanted to be sure to find a secluded campsite, because she had big plans for the night. When she started describing the things she was going to do to me, I became painfully excited. That was what she had in mind, of course. She continued teasing me until I felt like I would wet myself. Every now and then, she even reached over and stroked me through my pants to magnify my arousal.

Not to be outdone, I began describing the lewdest sex acts I could imagine, until I could tell by the way Karen was breathing that I was getting to her. We rode that way the whole time, kind of having a contest to see who could create the most erotic images with words. By early afternoon, we were both trembling with sexual excitement and eager to get camped.

We started looking for campground signs, considering several before we decided to stop. The one we chose was about three miles off the highway on a heavily wooded hillside. The dirt road that led to it was flanked by a riotous array of autumn wildflowers. I stopped the car for a moment and got out to pick a huge feathery pink blossom. When I got back into the car, I stroked Karen's face with it seductively. Then I touched it to each of her breasts and kissed it before handing it to her. When I drove forward, I knew that she was thinking about sex. And so was I.

At the entrance to the campground, there was a cabin with a sign on it that said OFFICE. Parking in front, I went inside while Karen waited in the car. In the office, a gray-haired man sat in an easy chair staring at the baseball game on TV. Without looking up at me, he said, "Guess you're not a baseball fan. Everybody else is home watching the game. You've got the place to yourself. Pick any campsite you want and pay me on the way out."

"We have the run of the place," I told Karen as I got back into the car. Driving slowly around the grounds, we looked for the ideal campsite. Each one was equipped with a picnic table, a water faucet, and a trash can. Even though there weren't any other people on the grounds, Karen was disturbed that the campsites were so close together. We kept cruising until we found a flat spot on top of a low hill. It was a little more private, because there was only enough level ground for two sites. We chose one of them, confident that we would have all the solitude we wanted.

The borrowed tent came with an instruction sheet, but it took me quite a while to figure it out and set it up. While I was doing so, Karen spread our picnic things on the table and inflated the air mattresses with a foot pump. When we both had finished, we put the air mattresses inside the tent and unrolled our sleeping bags, zipping them together to make a double bag big enough for the two of us.

We were sitting down at the picnic table to rest after our labors when a car passed the campsite, slowing down as it went by. Karen and I were worried about losing our privacy until the other car drove on. They were obviously inspecting the campground before selecting their spot, just as we had done.

A few minutes later, however, the car returned and pulled into the other campsite. I looked around to see whether the rest of the campground had suddenly gotten crowded, but except for the young couple in the car, we were the only people there. Karen and I looked at each other in disbelief. With all of the empty campsites, why did they have to pick this one? Their picnic table was directly across from ours. The way our tent was set up, they would be blocking our view no matter where they pitched theirs.

As they got out of their car, Karen whispered, "Should we move to another spot?"

Thinking about how much work it had been to set up the tent, I answered, "They might not be staying. Let's just wait awhile and see what happens."

"All right," Karen said, perhaps a little relieved herself that she wouldn't have to deflate and reinflate the mattresses. "But if they don't leave, promise me we can kill them."

We sat together watching sullenly as the other couple pulled a few things out of their car. They were both in their early twenties, clean cut, slim, and athletic-looking. They appeared to be a couple of college kids.

"Oh, shit," Karen said. "They've got a tent. They must be here to stay."

As the young woman unpacked a bag of groceries, her boyfriend began pitching a tent. It consisted of a canvas roof with four walls made of clear mosquito netting—the kind of tent that is usually used as an outdoor dining room. I was relieved.

"Don't worry," I told Karen. "Nobody sleeps in a tent like that. They're probably just here for a picnic. They picked this spot because of the view. I'm sure they'll be gone before dark."

The fellow had the tent up within minutes. By now his girlfriend had finished what she was doing and was sitting on top of the picnic table with her feet on a bench. He sat down beside her and kissed her lightly on the lips.

"Isn't that sweet," Karen muttered sarcastically.

I glanced casually up at them and noticed that the light kiss had turned into a passionate liplock. His mouth was pressed hungrily to hers, and his arms were wound tightly around her. I could see his tongue working its way into her mouth to duel with hers. I could even hear the soft moans of their passion.

I leaned toward Karen to suggest in a whisper that she take a look at the show, but she was one step ahead of me, obviously entranced by the physical display. I nudged her, and she turned her head slightly so that her curious stare would not be noticed. I could tell that she was still watching from the corner of her eye, though.

It was doubtful that the young couple would have seen us watching at that point, because their eyes were tightly shut and they were engrossed in each other. I must admit that I found the scene extremely exciting. I know that Karen did, too. My wife moved over next to me and rubbed her body kittenishly against mine.

As he kissed her, the young man placed his hands on the woman's chest. He pushed her gently backward until her back was flat against the table, her feet remaining on the bench. Continuing to kiss her, he began roaming freely over the swell of her bosom with his hands. I know I was openly staring now.

The woman made no objection as he cupped her breasts through her sweatshirt, slowly and languidly stroking each one. I could tell from the way the material outlined her nipples that she was not wearing a bra. He kneaded her flesh softly, bringing quiet moans of pleasure from her throat.

I looked at Karen to make sure that she wasn't missing the action. Now she too was openly staring, not even attempting a pretext of looking anywhere else. I turned back to the passionate couple, watching them candidly.

One of his hands moved slowly across her belly toward the waistband of her sweatshirt. As her body began to writhe slowly against the table, he slid his hand inside. Through the blue cloth of the sweatshirt, I could see his fingers closing over the mound of her firm young breast. My erection was straining against my pants, and there was nothing I could do about it. Nothing but stare at the unashamed display of lust.

I turned to look at Karen again and saw the expression on her face change suddenly. Quickly, I glanced back at our campsite neighbors just in time to see him pull up her sweatshirt, completely exposing her bare breasts. He stroked them lightly, rolling her bright pink nipples between his fingers. Then, leaning over her, he began to lick gently at the turgid flesh.

I hated to lose sight of her naked bosom, but his head blocked it from view for the moment. Without realizing, I put my arm around Karen's shoulders, feeling her melt against me. The young man began moving rhythmically from one nipple to the other, letting me see each of them in turn. They were wet with his saliva, glistening in the failing light of early evening.

He stopped sucking her breasts and began to nuzzle and kiss her face again. I heard them giggling and whispering to each other, but I couldn't make out what they were saying. They both glanced in our direction at the same time, catching us an instant before we managed to look away. From the corner of my eye, I saw the woman sit up and adjust her sweatshirt. To my disappointment, she was covering herself. I heard them laugh, and I was sure they were laughing at us.

The young lovers began puttering around their picnic table, preparing themselves some kind of meal. "Too bad the show's over," Karen muttered. "I was beginning to think they were actually going to *do* it right here and now."

"Well, I don't know about you," I said softly, although actually I did, "but I've seen enough to get me warmed up. *They* might not be doing it, but *we* soon will be. It's going to be dark soon. And then we're going to have some fun."

We started getting our own supper together without paying any more attention to the couple. I was sure that they would pack up and leave as soon as they had eaten. Although I wanted privacy, I was a little sorry that we wouldn't get to see more.

By the time we finished eating and cleaning up, it was almost dark. Karen helped me store our stuff in the trunk of the car, and then we went into our tent. Since it wasn't quite tall enough for us to stand up in, we crawled into the sleeping bag and wriggled out of our clothes. I left the tent flaps open so we would be able to look out at the sky and stars.

Our uninhibited neighbors had finished their cleaning up, and I fully expected that any minute they would take down their tent and pack up to leave. I was somewhat surprised when, instead, they got a pair of sleeping bags from their car and unrolled them on the floor of their tent. I could just make out their outlines in the moonlight.

"Looks like they're staying," I whispered to Karen. "Too bad it's dark, or I'll bet we'd really see something." As I spoke, the young man struck a match. In the light of the flickering flame, I could see them both clearly through the transparent walls of their tent. A moment later, the tableau was brightly illuminated. He had lit a lantern and hung it from one of the inside tent poles.

Karen and I stared wide-eyed as the woman undid the buttons of her boyfriend's pants and began pushing them down over his hips. He wore no underwear, and his semi-erect cock sprang immediately into view. He stood like that with his jeans halfway down his thighs while she stroked him to total hardness. Then he stepped out of them, drew his shirt off over his head, and posed totally naked.

Karen was trying not to show it, but I could see that she was fascinated by the sight of his organ. "It's big, all right," I whispered, to let her know that I didn't mind her looking. "This may turn out to be better than we expected." I could feel my wife's hand moving across my thigh, seeking my swollen penis.

We watched together as the man in the tent drew the woman's sweatshirt slowly off her. When she was naked from the waist up, she arched her back, thrusting her youthful breasts in our direction. She cupped the pale globes in her hands and lifted them slightly, as if offering them for our enjoyment.

"They know we're watching," I whispered to Karen. "They want us to see them. I'll bet that's why they picked this particular campsite."

"Do you really think so, Neal?" my wife asked, incredulous.

"Of course," I answered. "Just watch. If they really wanted privacy, they wouldn't keep the lantern on. I'll bet they don't put it out."

I was right. Without even turning their backs, they moved into each other's arms and embraced. We could see her breasts pressing flat against his chest, her pink nipples raking his skin. His hands were working on the buttons at the front of her jeans. As they kissed, he undid them and slipped the denim garment down over her hips. She wore nothing now but a wisp of red lace across her loins. The tiny triangle of material framed the white melons of her ass, pulling tight into the valley between them.

A moment later, he fell to his knees in front of her and pressed his face to her groin, slowly drawing the panties down her shapely legs. Her curling delta of venus was dark and mysterious, clearly visible to our gaze when he drew his face back for a long thorough look of his own. Then he pressed forward again, nuzzling at her sex with his nose and lips. From the expression of bliss that came over her face and the sounds of pleasure that issued from her throat, his tongue must have been probing her slit.

I heard Karen's breathing deepen as she pressed herself against me. Her hand was moving quickly up and down over my throbbing erection, bringing waves of sensation to my entire body. I could feel my wife's big breasts soft against my naked chest. I could smell the spicy scent of her arousal as we watched the young couple perform in the bright light of their lantern.

The woman bent her knees slightly to open herself wider, reaching down with both hands to grab him by the hair and pull his face more tightly against her. He held her buttocks in his hands, his fingers digging into the white flesh, kneading and squeezing as he drew her more firmly against him. She began to sob, twisting her face into a mask of passion.

"Oh," we heard her wail. "I'm going to come. Oh, yes, lick me. Oh, suck me. Oh, yes, I'm going to come."

Karen's fingertips were grazing lightly over the skin of my scrotum and the base of my penis, sending thrills of excitement all through me. She rolled onto her back and pulled me toward her, using my cock as a handle. I mounted her and moved my hips forward as she guided me into her.

When we looked across the clearing again, the woman was getting down onto her hands and knees. She was facing away from us, and we could look right into the open plane of her sex, her ass and pussy totally exposed to our hungry eyes. Some of the pubic hair grew back into her crack to frame the winking eye of her anus.

He stood over her, staring down at her nakedness and stroking himself casually, as if giving us a chance to get a good long look before mounting her. Then, squatting behind her, he held his stiff cock in his fingers and inched toward her. Because of the angle of their bodies, we could see clearly the tip of his erection approaching her open slit. Bending over her, he placed his hands on her shoulders and thrust his hips forward, doglike, to bury himself deep inside her.

We could see the end of his penis pressing against the lips of her pussy, spreading the wet flanges until the opening turned inward to accept him. Then, as we watched, his dick disappeared inside her in one long, slow, sinking stroke. Rhythmically, he moved forward and back, his testicles swinging with each motion. He increased the momentum of his thrusts until his sac struck her white skin every time he drove into her.

Unconsciously, Karen and I matched their bouncing rhythm. My wife's back arched and her hips thrust upward to meet my drives. Her legs wrapped tightly around my thighs. Our bodies melted together as we openly stared at the copulating couple.

The girl was sobbing and throwing her ass back at her lover. "I'm going to come again," she cried. "I'm going to come again. Oh, pump your come into me. Fill me up with it. Come with me. Come with me. Come with me."

Her words became a rhythmic chanting song that seemed to carry him to the point of orgasm. "Yes," he groaned loudly. "I'm going to shoot it to you." He made a sound like a wild animal caught in a trap and seemed to lose control of his body, bucking and thrusting violently.

At that very moment, I felt my own orgasm begin. I looked down at Karen and saw that she was looking back at me. "Yes," she whispered. "Yes, Neal. I'm ready, too."

As if her words gave me the permission I needed, I immediately began shooting my sperm inside her. Karen stiffened and relaxed, her body sending signals of climax that I had long ago learned to recognize. We got so wrapped up in our own orgasms that for a few moments we completely lost track of the other couple. When we looked at them again, the young woman was lying face down on her sleeping bag with her man on top of her. His cock remained buried inside her, but their bodies were still.

Karen and I dozed for a while. When we woke up a few hours later, the lantern in the other tent had been turned off, and the night was totally dark. We whispered softly about what we had witnessed until we were both tremendously aroused. Then we made love again. We made love twice more that night, stimulated by our voyeuristic experience. When the sun woke us the following morning, the young couple was gone, leaving no evidence that they had ever been there.

The campground remained pretty much deserted the next day, so we decided to stay another night. Several times during the day we slipped into our tent for more sex. Neither of us seemed able to get enough. Neither one of us could get the visions of what we had seen out of our minds.

THE BEST SEX I EVER HAD

To this day we talk about that episode whenever we want to add a little more excitement to our lovemaking. It has given us some pretty good times. But I'd have to say that the best sex we ever had occurred that World Series weekend when we camped and watched.

AWAKENING

Sonia's height is average, but nothing else about her is. Her braided, waist length hair is brunet with long waving streaks of natural platinum. Although she is thirty-five, she appears to be in her twenties. Her dark skin is smooth and flawless; her black eyes flash vivaciously. She smiles wistfully as she recounts the events leading up to her sexual awakening.

♥ ♥ ♥

I'm all grown up now and I've learned a thing or two. But when I got married at the age of twenty-two, I was like a child, as naive and innocent as they come. It's hard to believe that anyone could have lived through the liberated seventies without being exposed to sex, but I did. The problem was that there was no room in my upbringing for anything but religion. My mother says she had a rosary in her hand at the moment of my birth. I wouldn't be surprised if she was holding it at the moment of my conception, too.

I went to college, but I came out of it without knowing any more about life than I knew when I went in. I got my whole education from nuns and priests. At one point, I even thought I wanted to be a nun.

THE BEST SEX I EVER HAD

I met Philip when I was twenty-two. He was thirty-seven. Like me, he was Catholic, but he wasn't at all religious. His wife had been killed in an automobile accident. About two years after her death, he started dating. By the time I met him, there were lots of women in his life. He had even lived with some of them for a while. It's always been hard for me to understand why he was interested in me.

Philip says that my youth and innocence were what appealed to him in the first place. He had never met a girl like me; my virginity was a novelty. Now he claims that he knew all along that a sexual tiger hiding somewhere inside my pristine exterior was just waiting to be released. During the first year of our marriage, though, he must have developed some pretty serious doubts.

Prior to our wedding night, I had absolutely no sexual experience. Philip knew that, of course. What he didn't know was that I never even had sexual thoughts. I didn't think of sex as distasteful; I didn't think of it at all. I knew how babies were made, but that didn't seem to have anything to do with me.

Philip believed that he would introduce me to sex on our honeymoon, and I would blossom. He assumed that I would immediately find it as wonderful as he did. But that wasn't the way it happened. When I was faced with it, I discovered that sex frightened me. I was so inhibited that I wouldn't even let him see me with my clothes off. On our wedding night, I insisted on undressing in the bathroom and coming to bed in a long, shapeless nightgown.

I had been taught that it was my duty to satisfy my husband's sexual needs, and I was determined to fulfill that obligation. I actually thought I was doing so by lying on my back, pulling my nightgown up to my waist, closing my eyes tight, and spreading my legs.

I drew away when he touched my breasts because I couldn't understand what that had to do with his sexual needs. I think I held my breath while he thrust frantically inside me. I don't remember feeling any pain. I don't remember feeling much of anything.

Philip was patient. He was sure that within a short time I would lose my fears and inhibitions. But whenever he tried to make love to me, I lay stiff and tense beneath him, hoping that he would finish quickly. He didn't complain about it at first, but after several months he began to show his discontent. By the time a year had passed, he was regularly calling me frigid. Vaguely, I believed it was true, that I just wasn't built to enjoy sex.

One night, in a desperate effort to arouse me, Philip purchased a porno movie and insisted that I watch it with him. We sat together in our bed. When the opening credits flashed across the screen, I was a little curious about what I would be seeing. But when a couple appeared and removed their clothes, I became uncomfortable. When they started fondling each other's genitals, I was so embarrassed that I begged Philip to shut it off.

He got very angry and refused, complaining that I wasn't even willing to give it a chance. To embarrass me further, he started rubbing himself. He said that he could give himself a better time than I ever gave him. Humiliated, I ran from the room and sat weeping on the living room couch waiting for the movie to end. I fell asleep before it did.

When I woke up the next morning, Philip was still angry. Without saying a word to me, he slammed the door behind him as he left for work. I remained on the couch for a while, thinking. I was starting to realize that I had not been fulfilling my duties as a wife, that allowing my husband to stick his penis into me a few nights a week was not enough to satisfy his sexual needs.

Something in my girlhood training had been deficient. Mother taught me to cook and do laundry. In school, I learned how to add a column of figures so I could shop intelligently. But nothing had prepared me for sex. I didn't know what to do and I didn't know what to feel. I didn't understand what Philip could get out of watching a dirty movie, or why my refusal to watch it made him angry.

Perhaps I would understand better if I saw what it was about. Going into the bedroom, I found the videocassette on Philip's nightstand. With trembling fingers, I inserted it into the VCR and sat down on the bed to watch it. When the couple on the screen began removing their clothes, I forced myself to look. It was a little easier now that I was alone.

I tried to watch objectively as the woman undressed, even admiring the shape of her body as she revealed it for the camera. When the man began removing his clothes, I gazed in frank curiosity at his physique. In his brief underwear, he was muscular and attractive. When he was nude, and the camera moved in for a close-up, even his penis looked handsome.

I stared in silent fascination as he and the woman embraced and stroked each other. I could see that they were getting ready to have intercourse. But she didn't just lie back and spread her legs. She held his penis in her hand, petting it lovingly with a look of obvious pleasure on her face. I had never touched Philip there. Watching the woman on the screen made me wonder if maybe it would feel good to do that. She certainly was enjoying it.

I was hypnotized by the movements of her body, too. When I submitted to Philip's thrustings, I kept perfectly still. But the woman on the screen almost seemed to be dancing. Not only that, she appeared to be the aggressive partner. Placing her hand on the man's chest, she pushed him back against the bed and mounted him.

I looked on, dumbfounded, as she straddled him and used her fingers to guide his erection into her opening. Once it was inside, her hips started pumping rhythmically, matching his undulating movements with her own. His hands reached up to squeeze her breasts, and this seemed to increase her enjoyment. She moaned loudly as their bodies ground together. Philip sometimes made sounds like that when we were having intercourse, but I never did.

By the time the couple on the screen finished making love, there was a strange kind of tingling in my loins and breasts. I was sorry to see the scene end, but another began immediately. This time there was a woman alone. She was lying naked on her back with her legs spread wide, shamelessly displaying herself to the camera. While I watched in shock, she began caressing herself with her hands. When she stroked her breasts, her nipples became enlarged and hard.

Sometimes mine did that too, all on their own. Whenever it happened, I experienced a weird tingle. I wondered whether she felt that same sensation. Astonishingly, the things I was seeing were making me aroused. Since I had never known that feeling before, I was frightened by it. But to make sure the human race would survive, God must have made sexual excitement stronger than fear, even for a Catholic girl.

At that moment my nipples were so hard that they were actually aching. Curious, I pulled my nightgown off over my head and stared down, comparing my erect buds with those of the woman on the screen. Only half aware of what I was doing, I began stroking my breasts the way she was stroking hers.

When she started touching her genitals, I imitated those movements, too. I discovered that I could produce sensations that I never even knew existed. Before the movie ended, I had masturbated for the first time and experienced my first orgasm. It was the most wonderful experience I'd ever had in my life. Although I felt guilty, I couldn't help trying it again. The second orgasm was even more powerful than the first.

After that, I masturbated every day while watching portions of the porno movie. I progressed beyond imitation, devising my own techniques for self-gratification. I had orgasms consistently and discovered hidden erotic secrets about myself. Sometimes I wished that Philip could see me this way, that I could perform wantonly for him to demonstrate that I was capable of satisfying his sexual needs. But I was still too inhibited to share my discoveries with Philip. I simply couldn't imagine doing things like that while anyone, even my husband, was in the same room watching.

Anyway, he didn't show any sexual interest in me at all for weeks after the incident. When I tried to kiss him, he pushed me away, a look of frustrated disgust on his face. "What's the point?" he would mutter.

Now that I had found sexual pleasure, I feared that it might be too late. My husband was no longer aroused by me. He didn't reach for me at night anymore or attempt to make love to me. I worried that he might never want to again.

Then one afternoon, I got a crazy idea. Watching a woman masturbate on videotape had awakened my interest in sex. Maybe it could restore my husband's. Maybe Philip would be interested in me again if he saw a tape of me doing the things I had learned to do. The thought of it made me breathless. My inhibitions were beginning to melt.

I got the videocamera from Philip's closet and set it on the tripod, pointing it at the bed. Then I lay on the covers and began performing for the camera's eye. At first I felt somewhat awkward and clumsy. After a while, though, the thought of what I was doing added to the pleasure I was giving myself. My excitement overcame my embarrassment.

Afterward, I played back the tape I had made. Watching it aroused me all over again. My blood pounding, I tried to imagine how it would affect Philip. That evening, I didn't say anything to him about it until he started getting ready for bed. Then, popping the tape into the VCR, I hit the PLAY button and left the room.

Nervously, I sat in the living room, knowing that he was watching me do the most private and secret things a woman can do. The idea made me anxious and excited at the same time. After what seemed like an eternity, Philip came into the room. He was naked and there was a gleam in his eye that I had never noticed before. "Sonia," he said, "I never saw anything so sexy in my life."

For the first time, I stared openly at his erection. It was beautiful. How could I have gone so long without wanting to touch it? I reached toward him as he crossed the room. My excitement had been building ever since the day I first watched a couple make love on the television screen. While my husband had been in the other room watching me perform lewdly for him, the excitement had increased. I was ready for him at last.

When he stood before me, I stroked his manhood. I wanted him. I ached to feel his hands on me. I longed to guide his penis into my opening with my fingers, as I had seen the woman in the movie do with her lover. I even thought about kissing it.

That night, we made love on the couch and then on the living room floor before finding our way into the bedroom to do it again. I rose to heights I never imagined existed and had an orgasm every time. I wasn't skillful and I wasn't experienced, but I was willing. My inhibitions were leaving me forever, replaced by the discovery that sex with someone you love is a beautiful gift from God.

Since then I've learned a lot about the art of making love. Philip has learned a few things, too. I guess you might say that we both learned a few things, too. I guess you might say that we learn something new every time we lie in each other's arms. The night when I showed Philip my intimate videotape was a turning point. Over the years, our sex keeps getting better and better. Like vintage wine, it can only improve with age. But I guess the best sex is yet to come.

9

SEXUAL STARVATION AND EROTIC BANQUETS

One of the traits that characterizes a mature person is the ability to delay gratification. An infant empties its bowels whenever it feels the urge. A lion begins feasting as soon as it has killed. An adult human being waits until the time is right, however. When we are hungry, we go to the store for bread. But no matter how famished we feel, we don't usually eat it until we get all the way home. Even then, we are likely to wait until we have set the table and washed our hands.

There are many reasons why we are willing to postpone our pleasures. It may be healthier to wait for the right surroundings. It may be more comfortable or more decorous. It may be important to make efficient use of our energy by getting necessary business out of the way before settling back to relax. We may have to work so that we can afford to play. There are occasions, though, when putting off the good times is a way of enhancing our enjoyment.

After a three-day fast, a saltine cracker can seem like the best meal anyone ever ate. The starvation that sharpened our senses might have been imposed upon us by circumstances beyond our control. We might have been lost in the woods, for example, or suffering from an illness. On the other hand, we might have deliberately done without so that when finally we feasted we would better be able to appreciate the subtle flavors of our simple banquet.

Similarly, a bout with sexual starvation can make the erotic encounter that follows it feel like the most satisfying experience ever. Some people discover this by accident, after undergoing forced separation from their lovers. Others make a game of it, deliberately postponing sexual contact to increase their sensual fulfillment. The stories in this chapter are told by people who found that the best sex they ever had came after planned periods of abstinence.

THE WEDDING FEAST

Michael *is thirty-nine years old and has been a successful New York theater musician for more than half his life. He sports a sixty-dollar haircut, his shoulder-length hair carefully layered to preserve a well-groomed appearance. Its shiny black color contrasts dramatically with the steel gray of his eyes. He is lean and agile at a height of six-foot-two. A one-carat diamond stud flashes in his left earlobe to call attention to his masculine good looks. When we ask about the best sex he ever had, he wistfully recalls his wedding night, ten years ago.*

♥   ♥   ♥

I started playing the drums kind of late in life. I was eleven. Most pros start before they're seven. I learned fast, though, and was playing in a neighborhood rock band by the time I was fifteen. At nineteen, I got my first job on Broadway, in the orchestra for a hit musical. The show ran four years and I worked the whole time. When it closed, I got a gig with another musical right away. Since then, I've worked steadily, one show after another, with never more than a week or two between gigs.

That's how I met Sandy. It was about eleven years ago. I was twenty-eight, and she was twenty-seven. A friend of mine who was playing sax in a new show invited me to a party to celebrate the opening of rehearsals. It was at somebody's posh Park Avenue apartment, one of those open-house kind of affairs with people drifting in and out all night.

I noticed Sandy the minute she entered the room. You might say it was a case of lust at first sight. She had long, straight blond hair, the softest I've ever seen, and eyes the color of sapphires. She was tall and thin, with small breasts and tight little buns. Her curvy muscular legs tipped me off to her occupation.

I grabbed two glasses of champagne and headed straight toward her. "Welcome," I said, handing her a glass. "I bet you're a dancer."

She flashed me a smile that could have melted steel and looked me over carefully from head to toe. "And you must be a drummer," she answered, sipping the champagne.

"Hey, wait a minute," I said. "One look at those gorgeous legs told me that you're a dancer. But how did you know that I play drums?"

She smiled knowingly. "Maybe I'll tell you some-time," she said softly. "When we know each other better." Her voice was deep and husky, making her words sound like sexy music.

"Oh? Do you think we will?" I asked. My mind was racing, trying to remember whether I had ever met her before. I knew I couldn't have, because I never would have forgotten someone like her.

She wasn't coy or cutesy, like a lot of women would have been in that situation. She just looked me in the eye and said, "Yes. I think we will."

She was right, of course. We talked and laughed together for an hour or so, only half aware that there was a crowded party going on around us. After what I thought was a decent interval, I suggested that we go somewhere for a drink, and she immediately agreed.

We found a quiet corner in a cocktail lounge. When our drinks arrived, I said, "Well, do you think we know each other well enough yet? How could you tell I'm a drummer?"

Sandy affected an expression of mystery. "It might have been your hands," she said. "Or it might have been the rhythm of your movements. But probably it was when I saw you coming toward me with those two glasses of champagne, I asked a friend who you were, and she told me."

I laughed heartily. What a great sense of humor. We stayed in the lounge for a while to continue our conversation. Although we played at courtship sparring, we both knew how the evening would end. Within hours we were writhing in bed together in her apartment.

We went out again the next night and started seeing each other a few times a week from that point on. Sandy worked in the chorus of a musical a few blocks from where I played. We would meet for drinks and dinner after work and end up at her place, where we would make love until the wee hours. We started spending more and more time together. I found that when I wasn't with her, I was thinking about her and longing for her.

After only three months, I asked her to move in with me, and she accepted. Because her apartment was larger and more centrally located than mine, I actually ended up moving in with her. Everything was great, right from the start. We ate together, laughed together, slept together, and enjoyed life together. Every night after work at 10:30, we both rushed home to make passionate love.

There was something about our sexual communication that made it clear that we were right for each other. I'd been with a lot of sexy women before that. You know how show business is. But no other woman ever satisfied me the way Sandy did.

For one thing, I have a powerful appetite, always hungry for sex. Every night. Every morning. And in the middle of the day too, if I can get it. None of the other women I knew could keep up with me. Most of the time, after their first orgasm, they were ready to roll over and go to sleep. I always wanted more. Oh, some would try to accommodate me, but I could tell that their hearts weren't really in it.

With Sandy it was different. She had the same urgent sexual drive as I did. When she came back for seconds, I knew that it was because she wanted it as much as I.

I didn't usually go to work until evening, but she was rehearsing a new show and had to work all afternoon. Sometimes she'd call me from rehearsal to say that she was getting a break and heading home. When that happened, I'd wait for her, naked, in our apartment. As soon as she opened the door, I'd pounce on her, stripping off her clothes and scattering them around the room as I pulled her to the bed or dragged her to the floor. She didn't usually get more than twenty or thirty minutes off, so we'd start making love immediately and keep it up until the last possible second.

At night, we would have more time for leisure. Sometimes our foreplay would last for hours. We would take turns at massaging each other or kissing each other's bodies, until the kisses turned to oral sex. We would bring each other right to the edge of orgasm before stopping to switch roles. She satisfied all my urges, all my wants, all my erotic desires. And I knew I was satisfying her.

THE BEST SEX I EVER HAD

It wasn't just sex, either. We were deeply in love with each other. We both knew that it was only a matter of time before we got married. I brought up the subject of marriage after we had been living together for eight months. Sandy agreed at once, her eyes shining with tears of happiness. We set the date, reserved a ballroom in a Midtown hotel, and started inviting friends and families.

One night, about two weeks before the wedding, Sandy surprised me. As usual, I hurried home right after work, looking forward to several hours of steamy sex. But my fianceé had other ideas. When I arrived, she was still fully dressed. I noticed a suitcase in our apartment's entrance hall. I was horrified. Was she leaving me? Had she changed her mind about the wedding?

"Sandy," I asked nervously. "What's going on?"

"Don't worry, my love," she said in a voice that calmed me. "I've been thinking about something and I want to tell you about it.

"You see," she continued, "like every girl in the world, I always dreamed about my wedding night. I always wanted it to be something special. But the way we're living, it won't be special at all. We'll wake up together, have breakfast together, and get dressed together just like we do every day. Then we'll go to the wedding together and come home together afterward. Now what's special about that?"

I saw her point, but I couldn't imagine how she intended to change things. "I guess you're right," I said. "But that's life in the modern world. After all, we've been living together for almost a year. There's nothing we can do about that now."

"Well, in a way there is," she answered. "If we don't live together between now and then, our wedding night can seem like something special."

Now I understood the suitcase that I had seen when I came in. In a strange way it made sense, but I didn't like it.

"My friend Kathryn has a lovely apartment over-looking the river," she continued. "She left for Europe this morning and gave me her key. I've arranged for you to house-sit for the next two weeks."

I was stunned. "What?" I stammered. "You mean you're kicking me out?"

"Don't look at it that way, Michael," she said in a soothing voice. "Think of it as an investment in our future. After two weeks of not sleeping together, our wedding night will be so hot and sizzling that we'll remember it for the rest of our lives." As she spoke, she undid two of the buttons at the front of her blouse. I became hard at once.

"I don't know," I said, trying to sound logical. "Maybe there's a better way. I mean, two weeks seems kind of drastic. Suppose we just agree not to have sex for two or three nights before our wedding."

"No, no," she said in the husky whisper that had helped hook me on her in the first place. "I promise you a night that'll be worth waiting for. After two weeks without it, we'll be so turned on that there isn't anything we won't be ready to do." She undid another button and leaned over to lick my ear with the tip of her tongue.

"Let me tell you some of the things I have in mind," she whispered, reaching for my hand and placing it inside the open front of her blouse. I cupped her breasts, feeling her erect nipples poking against the inside of her bra. I was painfully hard, throbbing inside my pants.

She started describing the most exciting sex acts I could imagine, promising me a night filled with bliss. She told me exactly where she would put her fingers and her tongue. She told me about an erotic dance she was creating especially for the occasion, a dance that would arouse me more than I had ever been aroused. She promised to do things I had always dreamed of, and some I had never dreamed of. She alluded to positions so unusual that we had never even tried them before. All the while, she was blowing her hot breath in my ear and nibbling it. I was so turned on that I would have gone along with anything.

"Okay, my love," I murmured. "It's a crazy idea, but if that's what you want, I'll do it." As I spoke, I slipped my fingers inside her bra to search for the glowing ember of her nipple. Before I found it, Sandy pulled away from me, leaving my empty hand poised in midair.

"Quick," I said. "Let's go to bed right now. If it's going to be the last time until the wedding, I want to get started right away. I'll pack in the morning."

"No, my darling," Sandy said, rebuttoning her blouse. "This morning was the last time until the wedding. Your suitcase is already packed. Here's the key to Kathryn's place. The address is on this slip of paper."

"What?" I sputtered. "Why tonight? Why can't we just sleep together once more before this prison sentence begins?"

"No," she repeated firmly, opening the door. "You're out of here right now."

"But ..." Without quite knowing how it happened, I found myself standing outside the closed door of our apartment with a suitcase in one hand and her friend's key in the other. I turned to ring the bell but stopped myself, realizing that her mind was made up and there was no chance of changing it.

For the next two weeks, I went slowly crazy. We talked to each other on the phone two or three times a day, but never for more than a few minutes. She always managed to find some excuse when I asked her to meet me, saying that she was very busy at rehearsal or that she had too many other things to do. I missed her terribly and I was counting the days.

To make matters worse, I was horny as hell. Without any warning, I had gone from feast to famine. Sandy and I had been having sex several times a day, and suddenly I was on a sexual starvation diet. I tried jerking off, but that just didn't fill the bill. Once I even tried doing it while talking to her on the phone, figuring that it would be a little like making love. She knew instantly, though, from the sound of my breathing.

"Now, you cut that out," she said. Embarrassed, I stopped. As soon as we were off the phone, I finished what I had started, but it just wasn't enough.

I was beginning to find it difficult to sleep at night, tossing and turning for hours between twenty- or thirty-minute snatches of slumber. My erection never seemed to go away, and when I rolled around restlessly in my solitary bed, it pressed painfully against the mattress. I lost my appetite and was losing weight as a result. I never realized how sexual starvation could gnaw at a person day after day, night after night.

I couldn't even concentrate on my work. I beat out my rhythms mechanically, relying on reflexes that I developed in the year or so that the show had been running. Instead of thinking about the music, I was thinking about my erotic needs. The worst part was knowing that they wouldn't be fulfilled when work was finished or when the night was over. It seemed that I had been living like a monk for centuries, although it hadn't been quite two weeks. It was sheer agony.

By the time our wedding day rolled around, all I could think about was making love to Sandy. Never mind the ceremony. Never mind the reception. I wanted the honeymoon to start right away. I was obsessing. I was so hungry for sex that my body ached. I wasn't at all sure that I'd be able to get the pants of my wedding suit on over my hard-on.

I think I lost contact with reality for a while. In my mind, the wedding had turned into a night of lovemaking on a bed of passion. When I arrived at the hall and saw the room filled with guests, I realized that the consummation of our desires was still several eternal hours away. My brother, who was acting as my best man, thought I had the jitters because I was having second thoughts about getting married. Boy, was he mistaken. I wanted that ceremony more than anything I ever wanted before.

I don't remember much about it other than some hastily mumbled "I do's" and a voice pronouncing us man and wife. I had reserved a room in that very hotel and wanted to rush up to it as soon as the ceremony ended. But there was still that endless dinner and reception to sit through.

All the guests were eating and drinking and having a ball. Everyone but me. Food and dancing were the last things on my mind. All I wanted was to roll my bride in my arms, kiss her, and make wonderful love to her. When the band struck up "A Groovy Kind of Love," everyone called for Sandy and me to dance alone. As we glided across the floor, I held my wife tightly against me, fearful that the bulge of my erection would embarrass me.

"Let's get out of here," I murmured. "Everybody's having a good time. No one will notice if we slip away. Isn't that what newlyweds do?"

"Oh, silly," she said, giggling like a virgin. "We haven't even cut the cake yet." I could tell that she was enjoying the wait, pleased by my hunger for her.

Later, as our friends took turns proposing toasts to the newly married couple, I asked her again if we could leave. She shook her head coquettishly, saying, "Our guests, Michael. We mustn't forget our guests."

Finally, as the waiters were pouring coffee, she leaned over and whispered in my ear, "Now, my darling husband. Take me to our room and make love to me."

My knees were shaking as I stood and took her hand. Trying to be unobtrusive, I led her through the double doors to the elevators. My heart was pounding. I held her and kissed her as the elevator whisked us to the honeymoon suite. Opening the door, I lifted her and carried her inside. "Oh, God," I said. "Those were the longest two weeks in my life. I never want to go through anything like that again."

Sandy just smiled. "It will be worth it, darling," she said. "You'll see." With that, she stepped back and lifted the skirt and petticoats of her wedding gown, exhibiting the lacy garter belt that held up her stockings. I gasped. She was not wearing panties.

"I'm yours now," she said. "Come and take me."

I fell to my knees and pressed my lips to the milky skin at the tops of her thighs. As I kissed and nuzzled, she lowered the skirts so that I was inside the dress with her. Famished, I devoured her sex flesh. The moment my tongue touched her sensitive button, I heard her begin to groan rhythmically. She was coming already. Obviously, my bride was as hungry as I.

Without waiting to catch her breath, she stepped away from me as soon as her orgasm was finished and unzipped my fly. Holding my erection tenderly in her loving hand, she bent forward and took it into her mouth, bringing me to climax within seconds. Then she led me to the bed and guided me down onto it.

"We've finished starving," she said. "Now the real banquet will begin."

She began to dance for me, slowly and tantalizingly stripping off her clothing as she undulated to music playing in her head. The movements of her body were intensely erotic, bringing me to renewed erection almost instantly. When all her garments were removed, she danced naked, making age-old gestures with her hips and pelvis that seemed to say, "Fuck me, fuck me."

Her body swayed, arousing us both until we were ready to begin making love slowly and patiently, time after time, till night turned to day. Sometimes we came singly, one of us passive while the other gave pleasure. Then, immediately, we changed roles so that passive receiver became active giver. Sometimes we came together, striving in rhythm until the ecstasy of simultaneous orgasms made us fill the air with cries and sobs of satisfied desire. Even after that, we continued making love, moving without stop from one thundering climax to the next.

Sometime the following morning, we drifted off to sleep. We clutched at each other as if we both feared another separation like the one we had endured. When we woke, we loved again, trying desperately to make up for all we had missed.

That evening, we left for a short honeymoon in the Caribbean. During it, neither of us saw much of anything outside our honeymoon bedchamber, where we spent hours and hours each day and night satisfying our undying appetites. Our wedding night and the days that followed it were filled with the best sex either of us ever had.

There's no doubt that the period of sexual starvation prior to our wedding sharpened our desires and honed the cutting edge of our passion. Although we've been married for ten years, we haven't lost any of our sexual hunger. Sometimes, though, when we want to add a special spice to our life, we deliberately starve ourselves for a week or two. We talk about sex but refrain from all sexual contact until a predetermined day. Then we feast, indulging in an erotic banquet that always begins with Sandy's dance of the veils and never ends until our rapacious cravings are satiated.

WEEKEND SLAVE

Standing *five and a half feet tall, with a trim and shapely body, Gina makes a striking appearance. Her long hair is straight and jet black. Her green eyes are shaped like a cat's. Gina is an assistant editor for a young women's fashion magazine. She was divorced a little more than a year ago at the age of thirty-two. For the past several months, she has been seeing Frank, a radio disk jockey, on a steady basis.*

♥   ♥   ♥

My ex-husband and I were married when we were in our early twenties and hung together for almost ten years. It was awful. Thank God we didn't have any children; that would have made the divorce even messier than it was. There were lots of problems in our marriage, but sex was probably the worst of them. Lovemaking was never high on my ex's list of priorities. If I learned anything from my marriage, it was that life held no hope for sexual fulfillment. The closest I ever came to satisfaction was when I masturbated, which I did occasionally, but always with a great sense of shame and guilt.

Actually, until I met Frank, I didn't discover that my sexual appetites could be nourished. Frank is four years older than I am and went through a divorce just about the same time I did. When we met, I guess we were both hungry for companionship. Frank was mentioned in a story I was editing about radio personalities. When I called him to verify some facts, he invited me to lunch.

I was sexually attracted to him as soon as he sat down across the table from me. He was dark and mysterious-looking, with a compact body and very muscular hands. There was something in his voice that made it soothing and exciting at the same time.

Apparently, he was attracted to me too, because before lunch was over, he invited me to have dinner with him that same evening. Cautiously, I accepted. I was lonely, but after the horrible experience I had recently been through, I was unwilling to get involved in anything like a relationship.

We dined at a nice restaurant and shared a bottle of Beaujolais. I found Frank witty and entertaining. But when he suggested a nightcap at his apartment, I made up an excuse about having to get home early.

Frank laughed. "Let's face it," he said. "I'm trying to get you into bed, and you're turning me down." I was flustered, but he laughed again. "I'm just being Frank," he said. "How about dinner tomorrow?"

We went out twice more that first week and three times the next. Each time we did, Frank invited me to his bed, and I repeated my refusal. It may sound strange in this day and age, but I had slept with only one man. I was curious about how it would be with Frank, but I was convinced that all men were like my ex-husband, incapable of understanding a woman's sexual needs. After our tenth or eleventh date, my curiosity got the better of me. I agreed to accompany Frank to his place, but deep down I was expecting disappointment.

Frank surprised me. He was considerate and thorough. He kissed and caressed me until I was completely aroused. Then, slowly and artfully, he undressed me. Postponing the fulfillment of his own needs, he attended to mine.

His fingers found my most sensitive spots. His lips nibbled at all the right places. By the time he entered me, I was only a moment away from orgasm. After I came, he continued thrusting inside me until I was ready again. This time, he climaxed with me. When it was over, we lay together in silence, our arms and legs intertwined. I never knew that sex could be so good.

After that night, Frank and I saw each other regularly. Neither of us was ready to get involved in any kind of deep commitment, but I didn't go out with anyone else, and neither did he. We had dinner together almost every night. Afterward we made love, either in his place or mine. We occasionally spent the whole night together, but most of the time we parted, sleeping separately in our own apartments.

Frank was a wonderful lover. Sex wasn't just the ending to an evening out. He made it part of everything we did. Sometimes he would call me at work and whisper hoarsely about some fantasy that he was having. Other times he would describe things we did the night before, using that frenetic radio voice he usually reserved for announcing hits on his show.

He even found a way to turn sporting events into sex games. We're both ardent fans and we spend lots of evenings together watching sports on Frank's big-screen TV. Sometimes we make bets with erotic payoffs. If the shooter makes the basket, I have to give Frank a blowjob. If the batter strikes out, Frank has to go down on me for fifteen minutes without stopping. That sort of thing.

Steven and Iris Finz

Usually, we wait till the game is over before the winner gets to collect. By then the anticipation builds to heat up the session that follows. In fact, one of those bets led to the best sex I ever had.

It was a boxing match—a championship bout. The challenger was about fifteen years older than the champ, and I predicted that the champ would knock him out within the first three rounds. Frank insisted that the fight would go the limit and that the challenger would win it by a decision. I was so sure he was wrong that I was prepared to bet the farm.

In a flash of inspiration, Frank proposed the heaviest stakes ever. "A weekend," he said. "The loser has to be the winner's sex slave for an entire weekend."

"Okay," I said smugly. "You'll have to do everything I say from the time work ends Friday until midnight Sunday night."

Frank laughed. "It's going to be the other way around, I assure you," he said. "But let's make sure we have this straight. You're betting on the champ, and I'm picking the challenger. The winner will be master for the whole weekend. The loser is the slave and has to do everything the winner says."

"Agreed," I answered, certain of victory.

The match ended just as Frank said it would. He sat there grinning, his mind obviously working on the things he was planning to make me do. The idea of being his sex slave rather appealed to me. I found myself becoming aroused anticipating the erotic weekend that lay ahead.

We didn't see each other on Thursday because Frank had to work late at the station. On Friday, he called me at least fifteen times to remind me of my enslavement. The last call came just a couple of minutes before five as I was preparing to leave my office. He phoned to say authoritatively that I was to be at his apartment by six, ready to serve him.

In a seductive voice, I told him that I was looking forward to it. I was imagining a sort of romantic submission in which he put little silver chains on my ankles and made me wear a studded collar while I served him dinner in bed. Then he would make passionate love to me, forcing me to have one orgasm after another.

Frank had a different kind of slavery in mind. When I entered his apartment, he was sitting in an easy chair like a king on a throne. I started toward him for a hello kiss when, with a curt gesture of his hand, he commanded me to stop. "Right there, slave," he said. "Strip!"

I felt myself tingling all over. His voice was so harsh, his tone so dominant. He sounded so impersonal, ordering me to remove my clothes while he just sat and watched. I trembled with excitement and reached back to unzip my dress.

"Do it slowly," he commanded. "Turn around so I can watch the zipper come down."

The idea that he would enjoy something as simple as that aroused me tremendously. It made me feel sexy and desirable. I knew that I was in for an evening of erotic bliss. Facing away from him, I obeyed, unzipping as gradually as I could. I tried to picture the black lace of my bra and panties coming slowly into view. When I was ready to step out of the dress, he barked, "Now face me, slave girl. I want to see your tits."

The brutal tone of his command inflamed me. As I turned, I lowered the dress from my shoulders. When I looked at him, I saw that his pants were open. He had his cock in his hand and was stroking it slowly while he stared at me. Stepping out of the dress, I tossed it aside and awaited his pleasure.

"Take off the bra," he said. "And rub your nipples." Every word excited me.

Watching me wriggle out of my bra, he continued fondling his hard-on. My nipples, usually pink, were turning bright rosy red in my excitement. I had never performed this way before, not even in fantasy. Jolts of pleasure passed through me as I petted my breasts and twisted my nipples for his amusement. I could feel myself getting wetter and wetter under his hungry gaze.

"Now the panties," he commanded. "Take them off so I can see your pussy."

I found myself feeling a strange kind of delicious embarrassment. He had seen me naked many times, but this was different. I felt like a slave standing on the auction block for inspection by my master. Frank licked his lips greedily as I reached for the waistband to draw the delicate lace over my thighs. Stepping out of it, I stood before him totally nude.

"Now rub your pussy," he instructed. "Put your fingers in it and hold yourself open so I can see." He leaned forward, staring intently at my slit. "Move closer, slave girl," he added. "I want a good look."

I took two steps toward him and began rubbing my juices all over the pouting lips of my sex. I was feeling totally stimulated, absorbed in my erotic performance and in his erotic commands. My love button was hard and swollen. I hoped that he could see it peeking through. I pictured his tongue on it. I couldn't wait.

"Now rub your clit for me," he said. "And rub it good."

I started to comply, running my fingertips lightly in little circles around the sensitive nubbin. I hadn't masturbated since Frank and I got together; it didn't seem legitimate. But letting him watch me do it was different. It felt wonderful. I loved having his eyes on me while my fingers found my centers of pleasure.

"That will have to be enough," he said suddenly. "And I'm afraid it's all you're going to get until the weekend's over, my slave."

I was shocked. "You're kidding," I said. "Aren't you?"

He reached out to hand me something. "Not kidding at all," he answered. "Now put this on."

I never knew such a thing existed. It was a kind of corset made of black leather. The crotch was closed by a thick leather flap sewn onto the back and fastened in the front with a stout-looking brass lock.

"What is this?" I asked, incredulous. "A chastity belt?"

"Exactly," he answered. "To make sure the slave girl's pussy isn't touched all weekend. Now put it on and come here."

I struggled into the medieval garment and stood in front of him. He inspected it carefully, yanking on the lock to make sure it was properly closed. Leaning back in his chair he said, "Now, give me a handjob."

His cock was standing straight up through his open fly. I waited a moment, thinking that he would want to remove his clothes, but he sat there regally. Realizing that he expected me to service him just the way he was, I dropped to my knees before him. Taking his erect penis in my hand, I felt a thrill run through my body.

I know it sounds weird, but the idea of being his sex object and doing whatever I was told was marvelously arousing. I stroked him obediently, feeling his sex muscle swell against my fingers. Within moments, his come was spurting into the air. It was exciting to see him get off so fast.

"Very good," he said. "Now suck me till I get hard again."

Leaning over his lap, I felt the leather crotch-flap pull tight against my vagina. Every movement of my body caused it to constrict, erotically stimulating my sensitive membranes. I mouthed his flaccid penis while the heat built up inside me. The salty taste turned me on even more.

I licked him hungrily, certain that he would reward me with intercourse when I got him fully erect. It didn't take long for his cock to become turgid within the warmth of my mouth. When I felt it throbbing to full capacity, I drew back and touched the head lightly with the tip of my tongue.

"Don't you want to unlock this now?" I whispered. "I'd love to feel you in me."

"No way," he said. "You're my slave. Finish me with your mouth." Still believing that the evening would end with his hardness inside me, I tongued him to climax.

"I think I'll have you draw my bath now," he said when his orgasm ended. "Then you can bathe me, and maybe I'll even let you get me off again, in the tub."

I was beginning to think he was serious about not touching my pussy all weekend. By the time his bath was finished, I knew it was so. He made me lather his cock and balls with hot water and soap and rub him with slippery foam until he came again.

Throughout the weekend, I gave him orgasm after orgasm. I used every possible way that he or I could imagine, so long as my pussy wasn't involved. I played with his ass and sucked his cock. I stroked him with my fingers and with the soles of my feet. I held his hard-on between my tits and moved up and down until his hot sperm shot into my cleavage. I tickled his entire body with my long hair and blew hot breath on his genitals. I kissed his lips and his nipples while I jerked him off. He never so much as touched me. I was his slave entirely.

He made me wear the chastity belt all the time, even when we were sleeping. He unlocked it when I needed to use the bathroom, only to refasten it as soon as I was finished. The leather flap across my pussy stimulated me almost to the point of orgasm and kept me hanging there interminably. My arousal peaked and remained at the summit for hours at a time.

The sight of his swollen cock spurting into the air or onto my breasts and thighs brought me trembling to the brink of the abyss. The things I did to his body made my insides tingle with erotic hunger. Each moment took me higher, each submissive act further inflaming my passions.

Sometimes he let me think that he might be merciful and permit me to have a climax. Just a little one to tide me over. Once he even put the key in the lock on my chastity belt, sadistically changing his mind at the last minute. He teased and tantalized me, asking if I'd like to get fucked. I wanted to scream, "Yes, yes, yes. Please fuck me. Please oh please oh please." But I soon learned that he was immovable.

By Sunday evening, I was watching the clock and counting the hours. Although my erotic appetite was overwhelming, I actually enjoyed my role as obedient slave. I had never been in so intense a state of sexual excitement for so long a period of time.

For the past forty-eight hours, I'd been having sex in one form or another almost continuously. If I had been free to climax, it would have been over a long time ago. Instead, the sustained excitement was like an endless orgasm. Frank seemed to understand this and had a way of increasing my stimulation each time he came.

At ten P.M., Frank said, "You've been such a good slave that I think I'm going to reward you." When he fitted the key into the lock on my chastity belt, I thought he was taunting me again. But this time, he turned it and opened the lock. Pulling the flap open, he freed my hungry sex from its constricting prison. The fresh air bathed my moist membranes, caressing me like a lover's kiss.

Uttering a strangled groan, Frank fell on me, pressing his face against the damp cushion of hair that surrounded my pussy. He began kissing and licking me, his lips and tongue moving furiously up and down the length of my slit. He had been as hungry for my sex as I was for his. The moment the tip of his tongue found the button of my clit, I started to come. The sexual energy that had been building in me demanded release. My erotic hunger cried out as I gorged myself on the movements of his mouth.

My first orgasm was still bursting from my womb when I felt him carrying me toward my second. The waves of bliss were so potent that I tangled my fingers in my hair, trying to pull his face away so I could regain my strength. Heedless, he licked on, lifting my spirit to a plane of shuddering ecstasy. My passionate screams filled the air as climax followed climax, the second barely ending before the third began to build.

The muscles of my abdomen went tense, my back arching to lift my body off the mattress. I pressed my thighs to the sides of his head and bucked wildly against his nibbling lips and his thrusting tongue. Only after my fourth orgasm was spent did he let me fall back against the bed to rest for a moment before mounting me.

How could I take more after all those thundering climaxes? How could I possibly be ready to feel his cock inside me? How could I endure more stimulation so soon? Somehow I did!

As he slid slowly into my palpitating vagina, my excitement soared again. I was acutely conscious of the membranes of my sex parting before the onslaught of his plundering penis. He was filling me, stuffing me with the thick heft of his manhood.

All the waiting was worthwhile. Nothing had ever felt this explosively pleasurable before. I clawed at his back as he drove rhythmically in and out of me, each stroke taking me up another notch on the perilous climb to total release. I tottered at the edge, frightened of the final plunge. I felt my consciousness slipping away. I was merging with the cosmic flow, my juices floating me to nirvana.

For one aching moment, I clung desperately to the earth. Then Frank's thrusting cock tore me loose, casting me spinning through the vastness of erotic space. I thought my orgasm would go on forever. Totally unaware, I sang my pleasure to the heavens. Frank joined me, adding his manly groans to the harmony of our fulfillment.

Later, Frank carried me gently to the bath, tenderly lowering me into the hot water. Lovingly, he bathed me, soothing the sex muscles that had strained with pleasure until they were fatigued. Then, after drying me with a soft thick towel, he carried me to bed and held me in his arms until I fell into a smiling satisfied sleep.

We've had lots of good sex since then, and I'm sure there's lots more of it ahead of us. I'll never forget that weekend though. I starved for two and a half days in a state of excruciating excitement before feasting on the best sex I ever had.

10
EROTIC HOLIDAY

Every now and then a good engine needs to be overhauled. Worn parts are replaced, repaired, restored, or recalibrated. The exterior is repainted, and the switches are rewired. When the job is done, the device has, in a way, been re-created. Re-creation is the process of being brought back into existence.

When we apply the term to ourselves, we drop the hyphen and spell it *recreation*. Its meaning changes too, signifying the process of refreshing oneself with an entertaining activity. The change in meaning is only slight, however, because in refreshing ourselves we are, in a way, bringing ourselves back into existence. Without recreation, our spirits would run down like engines in need of an overhaul.

Intimate relationships occasionally need re-creation also. Lovers, or husbands and wives, may involve themselves so much in their individual activities that they lose touch with each other. Their schedules become so filled with work and family responsibilities that there may not seem to be time for a fulfilling sex life. Although sexual attraction probably played a role in bringing them together, they may forget it in the struggle to pay bills or maintain a lifestyle.

To keep passion from leaking slowly out of a love once charged with intense desire and emotion, some couples take an erotic holiday. They plan a night or weekend of sex the way other people plan a vacation. They select a particular date and location, making, in advance, whatever reservations are necessary. They arrange to have all business out of the way so that nothing will interfere with their amorous adventure.

Then, in a specially selected hideaway or in the privacy of their own bedroom, they devote themselves to lovemaking and romance. By forgetting the pressures of the workaday world and rediscovering sensual pleasure, they bring their stale relationships back into vibrant existence. Their sexual recreation becomes a true re-creation. People who have tried it say that their erotic holidays gave them the best sex they ever had.

GETTING OFF ON THE WEEKEND

Ellen *is five-foot-eight and quite thin. Her light brown hair is medium length and simply styled. At twenty-four, Ellen is the mother of two baby girls, ages one and two. In addition, she works part-time as a legal secretary. The combination probably accounts for the lines around her hazel eyes and the tired expression that she usually wears. Her husband, Chuck, makes deliveries for an overnight courier service and attends classes in the evenings in hopes of earning a bachelor's degree. Ellen says that she and Chuck have their best sex every few months, when they treat themselves to an erotic weekend.*

♥   ♥   ♥

It isn't easy having two babies so very close in age. Being a working mother makes it even harder. But these days, it's impossible for a family to live on just one income, so I really have no choice. Chuck helps out as much as he can, but between work and school he's hardly ever home. When he is, he has to study. I'm sure things will get better when he finishes school. Until then, this schedule is hell on our sex life.

Chuck and I started going out together when we were in high school. Everybody thought we made a perfect couple and assumed that we would get married after graduation. I guess I assumed it, too. That's why I didn't feel any guilt when we started having sex in our senior year.

The first time we did it was on the couch at Chuck's house. We were studying together when his parents said that they were going out for the evening. As soon as they left, we started hugging and kissing. As usual, I let Chuck open my blouse and bra so that he could play with my breasts. Before long, I was completely undressed and Chuck's hands were all over my naked body. It felt so good that I wanted to touch him the same way.

With frantic fingers, I plucked at the front of his pants in an effort to get them open. Chuck was surprised, because although he had frequently undressed me, his clothes always stayed on. This time it was different. I got his dick out and began stroking it exuberantly. Within minutes, he too was naked.

We grabbed at each other roughly, excited to be going so far at last. Artlessly, we rolled around until he was on top of me, his erect cock poised at the opening of my pussy. Hesitating for the briefest possible instant, we simultaneously lunged toward each other. I felt his erection tear into me, filling my loins with pain. I started to scream, but his mouth was pressed so tightly to mine that nothing came out but a muffled cry.

Chuck, oblivious to my suffering, humped away until he was buried to the hilt inside me. Just as the pain of his entry was beginning to subside, he moaned and started his climax. Seconds later, he was lying by my side panting in an effort to catch his breath. When I saw streaks of bloody semen on my legs, I cried. My virginity was a thing of the past.

We agreed that it had been a mistake that we

wouldn't repeat until we were older and more settled. But two hours later, we did it again. This time it didn't hurt, and the fuck lasted a lot longer, although I didn't have an orgasm. Since I didn't know what to expect anyway, I wasn't disappointed, and it did feel good.

After that we did it every chance we got, learning more about each other's desires and needs as we went along. We got better and better at it, and it felt more and more wonderful. By the seventh or eighth time, I was getting close enough to orgasm to realize that it was supposed to happen. A week or so after that, I climaxed with him. I couldn't wait for graduation so that we could be married.

When school ended, Chuck started acting strange. I realize now that he wasn't ready for marriage. The prospect frightened him. Every time I brought it up, our discussion would end in an argument. After a while, he seemed to be looking for excuses not to see me. A few months after we graduated, Chuck said that he needed a break from our relationship. He said he thought it would be best if we tried dating other people.

My mother always told me that a girl shouldn't have sex until marriage because if she did the guy would have no reason to marry her. "Why should he buy the cow," she had said, "if he can get the milk for free?" It was beginning to look like she was right. Chuck and I stopped seeing each other.

It wasn't until a year and a half later at a party that we ran into each other. In the meantime, I had dated a few other guys, but never even came close to having sex with them. When I saw Chuck at the party, my heart started to flutter. I stayed as far away from him as I could because I was sure he no longer had any interest in me. He came over to where I was standing, though, and asked me to dance.

While we were dancing, he said that he had been missing me a lot and wanted to call me but just didn't know what to say. We danced every dance. After the party, we went out for a soda. We started dating again, and within six months, we were married.

At first our life together was like a vacation. Chuck drove the delivery truck and I worked as a secretary. At the end of each workday, we rushed home to our tiny apartment to have sex, and then to have dinner, and then to have sex again. We didn't have much money, but that didn't matter. We made beautiful love, and that was enough for us.

Most of our friends were still single and lived with their parents. As a result, they had money to spend on shows and entertainments. We didn't need that, because Chuck and I made our own entertainment. Sex was our pastime. We elevated it to a high art by making up games that indulged our fantasies.

One night, for example, I came home from work to find the apartment dark and unusually quiet. When I turned on the light, I was startled to see Chuck with a toy pistol in his hand, his face completely hidden by a ski mask. Before I had a chance to say anything, he leaped behind me and put his hand over my mouth. Holding the toy pistol to my head, he said, "Behave yourself or I'll kill you."

Falling right into it, I acted scared. "Please don't hurt me," I begged. "I'll do anything you say."

At gun point, he ordered me to lift my skirt and pull the crotch of my panties to one side. Then, forcing me to lie on the kitchen table, he opened his pants and stuck his cock into me. He fucked me without removing a single article of clothing from either of us, keeping the pistol pointed at my head the entire time. After he came, he pulled out of me, zipped his fly, and left the apartment. When he returned half an hour later, he acted as if nothing had happened.

Another time, I borrowed some clothes from a girl-friend who was smaller than I was. I changed into them before leaving work. When I arrived at our apartment, I was wearing black fish-net stockings and a short black leather skirt that was so tight I could barely walk. I had removed my bra and wore a tight, low-cut red sweater, which showed my tits practically down to the nipples.

Instead of letting myself in with a key, I knocked. I heard Chuck call, "Who's there?"

I answered, "Escort service." When Chuck opened the door, the puzzled look on his face changed slowly into a grin of understanding.

"You called Ellen's Escorts?" I asked, wriggling my shoulders to move my breasts from side to side. "I'm here to serve you. Pay in advance, please." I took the ten-dollar bill that Chuck extracted from his pocket, slipping it into my cleavage. Then, stepping inside, I said, "Drop your pants, please. I don't have much time."

Obediently, Chuck undid his belt and let his pants slip down to his ankles. His cock was already erect and straining at the taut fabric of his white briefs. Abruptly, I pulled down his underwear to free it. Without another word, I dropped to my knees and took his prick in my hand.

I rubbed it up and down roughly, trying to simulate the callous movements of a paid hooker. When I felt it bulge with excitement, I gently licked its head with the tip of my tongue. I nibbled up and down the shaft until Chuck's breath was coming in labored pants. Then, without any further ceremony, I took the length of it into my mouth and started sucking voraciously.

I bobbed my head back and forth in a fucking motion, trying to bring him off as quickly as possible.

When I felt him swelling in preparation for ejaculation, I pulled my mouth away and finished him by stroking him to climax. Before his cock was completely soft, I stood up and said, "Thank you. Call again."

As the apartment door closed behind me, I could hear him saying, "Hey, where are you going?" I returned about twenty minutes later carrying a pizza. I bought it with the ten dollars that he paid me for the blowjob.

Just when I was beginning to think that we would share these moments of erotic bliss forever, I discovered I was pregnant. We were both thrilled, of course. But I don't think either of us realized the change that a baby would bring to our lives.

For the first few months of the pregnancy, we were more active sexually than ever. Chuck said that my rounded belly and enlarged breasts turned him on. That turned me on. Chuck bought a plastic vibrator, which brought us many pleasures. We spent hours playing with it and fucking almost every night. We invented new sex games, tailoring them to fit my blossoming condition.

As the time for my delivery came closer, I found myself feeling clumsy and ungainly. After I stopped working, our sexual activity decreased drastically. Then Helen was born, and sex went out the window. At first, it was because I lost interest. But even when I started wanting it again, we just didn't have time.

The baby seemed to require all my energy and attention. She never slept and was always demanding to be fed, held, or changed. It was all we could do to steal a quick fuck before going to sleep at night. Neither of us ever really felt satisfied.

All too soon, I became pregnant again. Shortly after Charlene was born, we realized that we wouldn't be able to survive financially unless I returned to work.

When I went back to my old job on a part-time basis, it began to look like we would have to give up sex completely. The girls were so close in age, and little babies are so needful, that it was all I could do to keep up with them.

Chuck started going to school at night. With school, our jobs, delivering the babies to and from day care, and taking care of them when we were home, neither of us had the strength or the time for sex. Not that we stopped wanting it. Not by a long shot. I remember sitting at my typewriter at work staring into space and thinking about the days when Chuck and I used to make love all weekend long. I imagined complex erotic scenarios, remembering games we had played and inventing new ones in my head.

One evening, when he had a break between classes, Chuck called me to see how the kids were. I had been having a sex fantasy. It involved handcuffs. I was so horny that I asked Chuck to cut school and come home to fuck me. "Sorry, love," he said. "You know I can't do that. I've got to run or I'll be late for class."

"Wait," I implored. "I've got a real hot idea." I tried to tell him about my fantasy, but he cut me off.

"No time now," he said. "Write it down or something. I'll read it when I get home."

I was frustrated, but I couldn't blame him. Life was just as hard for Chuck as it was for me. Remembering his suggestion, I got a sheet of paper and began describing a bondage fantasy, complete with manacles, shackles, whips, and chains.

Later, when Chuck got home, he was too tired to read it. "Drop it in there," he said, gesturing to a glass vase on the nightstand. "I'll read it in the morning." By then I was so tired that it didn't make any difference anyway.

271

The next morning when Chuck did get around to reading it, his face took on a wistful look of excitement. "This is great stuff," he said. "Too bad there's never time anymore. But let's save the idea." Suddenly his face lit up. "Why don't we store our fantasies in this little vase? That way we'll be ready whenever opportunity knocks."

That was the beginning of our new sex game. I wrote my desires down on slips of pink paper and Chuck wrote his on blue. Most of the time, we put them directly into the vase without showing them to each other. After a few months, the vase was filled to the brim. Sometimes we speculated about whether there were more pink slips or blue ones.

One night, Chuck tapped the vase and said, "I think it's time we did something about this collection."

"I think so, too," I said. "But what?"

He told me that he had arranged for his mother to take the girls the following weekend. "We'll take turns drawing slips of paper out of the vase," he said. "I'll pick the pink ones and you'll pick the blue. We'll have to do whatever the fantasy requires."

It seemed like the weekend would never arrive. When it finally did, I was all worked up. I waved as Chuck's mother drove off with our children in her car. As soon as she was out of sight, I turned to look at Chuck. He was grinning lewdly, the glass vase in his hand.

"Let's go into the bedroom," he suggested in a whisper. "I'll do one of yours." He shook the vase and reached in to draw out a folded slip of pink paper. As he read it, a slow smile spread over his face. Passing it to me, he went to the closet.

I glanced at the words I had written, probably six weeks before. "Tie me to the bed and don't untie me until I've had three orgasms." When I looked up, Chuck was standing in front of me with four neckties in his hand.

I quickly undressed and lay back on the bed, spreading my arms and legs so that he could bind my wrists and ankles to the four corners of the bed frame. When he was done, I pulled at the ties to see whether they would really restrain me. I was truly a prisoner in my own bed.

Lying naked and helplessly pinioned, I felt totally vulnerable. Chuck could do anything he wanted to make me come. There was nothing for me to do but lie there and take it. I tingled all over with excitement. Wide-eyed, I watched him remove his clothes to stand by the side of the bed looking down at me.

His cock was stiff and swollen, sticking straight out in front of him. I could see a vein in its shank throbbing rhythmically. Slowly, he stroked its length as his eyes roamed over my bound body. I could tell that he was considering all the things he would do to me.

Sitting beside me on the mattress, he placed his hands gently on my shoulders. He cupped them before trailing his fingers softly over my arms all the way to my wrists. The lightness of his touch was tantalizing. I could feel my nipples stirring, the dark disks that surround them crinkling with excitement.

He leaned over and, without touching them, breathed warmly on my erect pink buds. At the same time, his fingers explored my armpits and strayed down my sides, caressing the ridges of my ribs and meandering over the prominences of my hips. His hands traveled over my nude body in a random pattern, one tickling the crease under my breast while the other traced the contours of my calf or thigh. I felt my pussy becoming damp as his strokes aroused my desire.

His hands mounted my breasts and circled closer to my nipples. I wanted him to grasp and squeeze them, to twist and rub them, but he continued to tease me. I heard myself sigh as he cupped one breast. I moaned as his hand traveled on. His fingers were tracing figure-eights across the plane of my belly, making little designs around my sensitive navel and dipping to a point just above the line of my pubic mound.

He began moving the fingers of one hand in spirals around my pussy, driving me frantic with longing. Arching my back, I tried to press myself upward against his tormenting hand. I wanted to feel his fingers inside of me. I wanted it desperately.

He was teasing me with both hands now. One was toying gently with the curls of my pubic hair, venturing to twirl a few strands around his fingers before retreating to the softness of my abdomen. The other hand was stroking the insides of my thighs, reaching under me to swab a probing fingertip against my puckered anus.

His touch came closer all the time to my heated center of desire, but still he held back. If I hadn't been tied down, I would have thrown myself at him, wrapping my arms and legs tightly around him, forcing him to satisfy my needs. But I was helpless.

My pussy dripped moisture, the fluids of my excitement dampening the pink folds of flesh that guarded my opening. I was possessed by an insatiable need for fulfillment. My clit was swollen and erect, hard as a ruby and begging for attention. I knew instinctively that it was peeking out from under its protective hood, all red and glistening.

His fingers passed lightly over the lips of my pussy, bringing their heat to the nerve endings of my pleasure center. His fingers came closer. Closer. Maybe he was making contact. Maybe he was touching me; I wasn't sure. Yes. His fingers were sliding alongside my clit, pressing my own flesh against it. I felt the erect little nubbin grow thicker, harder. Then the tip of his finger grazed its head and I felt myself explode. I wailed as my body gained release from the sexual tension that had been building for so long. Was it minutes? Or was it months?

My eyes closed tightly. I rolled my head from side to side, rocking under the flashes of heated exhilaration that ran through my body. I gasped for breath, sobbing and whining with pleasure. As my climax reached its zenith, I slipped over the edge, drifting back to earth as though suspended from a huge satin parachute.

A long time later, I opened my eyes to Chuck's smile of satisfaction. "That's one," he said. "You still have two to go. This time, I'll get right to the point." Reaching into the night-table drawer, he brought out the white plastic vibrator, which we had almost forgotten. He held it in front of my face for a moment to give me a preview of my next pleasure. Then he flipped the switch to start it humming.

In contrast to the teasing slowness with which he first aroused me, he placed the vibrator's tip against my clit immediately. Although it had been at rest, the little organ sprang to life at once, reaching instant erection. Chuck held the vibrator directly on it, moving the device in small circles, keeping it always in contact with my pulsating button.

I didn't believe it could happen so fast the second time, but it did. Clouds of orgasm started forming within moments. Once they broke, there was no stopping the torrent. I seemed to be coming forever, my consciousness buffeted by the storm of erotic ecstasy. When it was over, I issued a satisfied sigh.

Chuck turned the vibrator off and began stroking

the outer lips of my pussy with its silent tip. "No, Chuck," I begged. "Not yet. It's too soon." I wanted to snap my legs together to gain a moment's rest before he started on me again. But the ties that bound me to the four corners of the bed made it impossible. There was nothing for me to do but take all the stimulation he offered.

I felt him slip the plastic cylinder between the lips of my pussy, fucking me slowly with it. Involuntarily, I rocked my pelvis up to open myself for it. Incredibly, I wanted more. I wanted to feel it all the way in me. Sensing my need, Chuck moved it steadily deeper, filling me with the thickness of the sex toy.

When it was buried as far as it would go, he stroked it in and out as if it were his cock. I clenched the muscles of my groin, tightening the walls of my pussy around it, increasing the friction. I watched as he bent lower until, at last, his lips were pressed to my clitoris, already erect again. Just as he sucked the throbbing button into his mouth, he turned on the vibrator.

I was overwhelmed by the flood of sensations that filled my rocking pelvis. I felt myself being fucked and licked at the same time, every nerve of my sex tingling with stimulation. Loudly, I filled the air with my passionate cries. Another orgasm was building in my humping loins.

The flowing juices of my arousal bathed my clit as Chuck ran his tongue tip over its head again and again. The combination of his licking and the persistent vibrations inside my womb brought my climax rupturing forth. Tearing through the wall of resistance, it filled my body with shuddering spasms of sexual fulfillment.

When my third orgasm ended, I fell back against the pillows and breathed deeply. I was completely satisfied, and yet I felt ready for more sex. Now I wanted to please Chuck the way he had pleased me. I wanted to bring him to the urgency of explosion by fulfilling one of his dearest fantasies.

After a short rest, my husband untied me, and I reached into the vase for one of his blue papers. Following its instructions, I smacked his ass repeatedly until it glowed bright red and then sucked him until he soared. After that, he drew another pink paper. And after that I drew another blue. When the weekend was over, the vase was half empty.

Waiting for Chuck's mother to arrive with the babies, we agreed to have another erotic fantasy weekend as soon as possible. Since then, we've managed to spice up our life by devoting every seventh or eighth weekend to sex games. For us, these erotic holidays lead to the best sex ever. They give us something to look forward to as we write our fantasies down on slips of paper and refill the vase with them.

ANNIVERSARY

Henry *is forty-nine years old with a sprinkling of silver in his brown hair. He is five feet eleven inches tall and slightly overweight. His lively gray eyes are surrounded by laugh lines which make him appear to be perpetually smiling. Henry is a dentist. He reveals two perfect rows of gleaming white teeth as he talks about the twenty-fifth anniversary of his marriage to his wife, Yvette.*

♥ ♥ ♥

It may sound funny, but the idea for this adventure came to me one day about two years ago, while I was drilling a patient's tooth. If you aren't a dentist, you can't possibly imagine how dull and uninteresting it is to spend your whole day filling cavities. You smile and tell the patient that it isn't going to hurt a bit. Then a quick shot in the gums and it's drill, drill, drill.

This goes on for eight or ten hours a day, every day of the week. By the end of the afternoon, all I feel like doing is going home and flopping down in front of the TV set. But maybe life is like that. I don't know. You get older and your practice gets more successful and you find you just don't have time anymore to stop and smell the roses. Yvette understands and never complains about it, but I'm sure she can't help feeling a bit neglected.

We don't even have sex as often as we'd like to. And when we do, it's too much like some obligatory activity that we've managed to work into our busy schedules. For me, the best kind of sex is the romantic kind, where you build up to it slowly so that it truly feels like an act of love instead of just a mechanical coupling. But we don't seem to have time for that anymore.

It wasn't always like this, of course. When Yvette and I met, we were both going to school in New York City. New York is a noisy, dirty, crowded metropolis, unlike anything here on the West Coast. But in spite of the hustle and bustle, you can find romance if you know where to look for it.

I remember one summer evening when I surprised Yvette with an al fresco candlelight dinner right there in the heart of the city. I cooked and served her a lavish meal on a table that I set up on the roof of the apartment building I lived in. I borrowed some decent china and a tablecloth to create a feeling of luxury. Yvette acted like we were in the best restaurant in town.

Afterward, in my apartment, we made beautiful love. I'm not just talking about sex. I'm talking about making love. That sense of romance is what makes all the difference. We used to fill our lives with romance back then. Sometimes, when it was raining, we'd drive to the beach and just sit in the car holding hands and enjoying the stormy ocean waves. We might kiss and pet a little to warm ourselves up for the night of passion that was sure to follow.

It's a good thing romance doesn't cost much, because I didn't have any money to speak of in those days. That never stopped us from having a good time, though.

I remember once when we spent an entire Saturday afternoon sitting together in a bathtub full of bubble bath and drinking champagne. It was cheap stuff, but we knew how to make the best of things. I think we must have made love four times that afternoon, our bodies slipping and sliding in all that soapy water.

Well, about a year ago, there I was working on a patient when I started daydreaming about the way Yvette and I would set aside a whole day or night for romance and making love. I found myself wishing things could be like that again. I realized that our twenty-fifth wedding anniversary was a few weeks away, and decided to do something to recapture those old feelings. We usually celebrate our anniversary by going out to dinner and maybe the theater. But this time, I made up my mind that the theme for our celebration would be romantic lovemaking.

I remembered an ad I had recently seen in one of those slick magazines devoted to the affluent lifestyle. The ad was for a resort that described its accommodations as "luxury honeymoon cottages." I thumbed through all the magazines in my waiting room until I found the one I was looking for and called to inquire.

The reservations clerk told me that each of their cottages faced the ocean and was laid out in a way that took best advantage of the ocean view. They all came with redwood hot tubs, platform beds, and patios. The atmosphere sounded exactly like what I had in mind. The rates were exorbitant, almost a thousand dollars a day, but Lord knows I can afford it now.

That night I asked Yvette how she would feel about celebrating our anniversary by devoting the night to sheer sexual ecstasy. I told her about my yearning for our old sense of romance and my hope that we would find it in the honeymoon cottage. It seemed to be just the kind of thing we would have done when we first met, if we weren't always so broke back then. Yvette jumped at the idea and said that she too longed for the kind of lovemaking that used to come so easily to us when we were younger. The next morning I called to book the cottage.

As the day approached, Yvette and I became even more enthusiastic about the idea. I shopped around for a beautiful diamond necklace to give her as a gift. The night before we were to leave, I went to the best department store in town and also bought her a luxurious negligee. It was white satin, trimmed with delicate white lace, and reminded me of her wedding gown. The memory of Yvette as a bride increased my feeling of romance.

On the day of our anniversary, I had a local florist fill the back of my car with flowers. There must have been hundreds of them. I wanted the fragrance to surround us completely as we drove to our romantic rendezvous. When Yvette got into the car and saw them, she gasped with delighted surprise, her blue eyes gleaming.

We took a leisurely drive, meandering our way up the coast. To our left, the ocean was a brilliant cobalt blue. To the right were rolling hills of bright forest green. It all contrasted dramatically with Yvette's long golden hair. Everything was perfect. All I could think of was the hours we would soon be spending in each other's arms making passionate love.

It was late afternoon when we arrived at the cottages. A uniformed valet assisted Yvette out of the car. While we checked in, he drove the car to our cottage and brought the flowers into the room. Another valet transported us to the cottage in a horse-drawn buggy with seats of soft brown leather.

The cottage itself was nothing short of magnificent. It was completely surrounded by trees, creating the feeling of total privacy. The valet opened the intricately carved mahogany door and conducted us inside. The room was beautiful. It was made for lovers.

The first thing we noticed was the view. The wall facing the ocean was glass from floor to ceiling, with nothing to obstruct our vision. The blue water seemed to begin at our feet and to stretch endlessly, until it faded into the misty horizon. Sea birds flew lazily by, their hoarse calls in harmony with the ocean's musical roar.

Our suitcases had been unpacked for us, and the flowers arranged in vases throughout the luxurious room. The art-deco furnishings were sparse, accentuating the importance of the huge platform bed that occupied the center of the room. Recessed into the floor next to the glass wall, a redwood hot tub was already filled, the warm water steaming and bubbling, inviting lovers to partake of its sensuous delights.

As the valet left, he handed me a menu and said, "You may call to order dinner, sir, whenever you are ready."

As soon as we were alone, I took Yvette in my arms and embraced her. I was already aroused by the thought of what lay ahead, and the warmth of her tall slender body increased the effect. I was beginning to feel a stir in my trousers. When Yvette pressed her lips to my ear and whispered, "It's lovely," I wasn't sure whether she was referring to the room or to my obvious erection. "I'm so glad you brought me here."

"I wanted it to be special," I whispered. "And I have something very special for the occasion." I handed her a gilt-wrapped package that contained the negligee I had purchased.

"Ooh, Henry, I love it," she said as she removed the lacy garment from the box. "I can't wait to wear it."

"Why wait, then?" I asked. "Why don't you put it on now? I'd love to see you in it."

A few minutes later when she emerged from the dressing room wearing the opulent lingerie, I sighed lovingly. "You look beautiful," I murmured. "Seeing you in that gown brings back our wedding night. It was twenty-five years ago today, but it seems like just last week. And I'm just as excited about possessing you tonight as I was then."

"Oh, Henry," she replied. "You make me feel young and vibrant. We're going to make wonderful love tonight. Nothing could make it better."

"Well," I said slowly. "Maybe something could." As I spoke, I stepped behind her, slipping the diamond necklace from my pocket. I guided her to the mirror so that she could watch as I put it on her. When the jewels were sparkling at her throat, she turned and kissed me again, this time with a burning passion that drove the tip of her tongue to flick lightly over my lips as a promise of things to come.

By the time our sumptuous dinner arrived, the sun was beginning to set over the Pacific. Three waiters came to our room and prepared a table by the window, setting it with fine bone china and Waterford crystal. Before leaving, they placed the food on our plates and lit candles in highly polished silver holders. We gazed at the sea as we dined on chateaubriand and sipped a rare vintage cabernet.

As the waiters reappeared, we heard the strains of soft music. On the beach outside our window, a trio was playing a serenade for lovers. Yvette reached across the table to squeeze my hand. "You're wonderful, Henry," she murmured. I felt myself stirring to erection again.

We watched the waiters prepare our crepes suzettes with movements that seemed choreographed to the music playing outside. Yvette's face shone in the illumination of the flaming dessert, the dancing shadows playing over the curves of her body in the satin negligee. I couldn't wait for the waiters to leave. I wanted to hold her in my arms.

When they were gone, I rose from my chair to stand behind her, stroking her hair and shoulders as she fed herself and me with alternate bites of the crepes. My excitement was rising. From the deepened rhythm of her breathing, I could tell that she too was becoming aroused. I slipped the fingers of both hands into the bodice of her negligee, tracing the curves of her rounded breasts. I heard her sigh.

Standing, she turned to face me and melted into my arms. Instinctively, our hips began grinding, pressing our pelvises together as we embraced. Her skin was soft and smooth, crying out for my caressing touch. "Thank you for being my wife," I murmured, moving my hands slowly over her body to find the softness of her buttocks and her breasts. I felt like a horny young kid again.

Without breaking lip contact, I eased the straps of Yvette's negligee off her shoulders. She wriggled sensuously until the garment slid down her body to form a satin and lace puddle on the floor around her ankles. Moonlight streaming in through the window highlighted the swelling curves of her bosom. In the dim illumination, I could see the rosy disks of her nipples contracting to stand erect at the ends of breasts that were still remarkably firm and youthful. I fell to my knees and pressed my face against them.

I licked her turgid blossoms, closing my lips over each of them to suck lightly. I could feel my manhood swelling within the confinement of my clothing.

I wanted to be naked, as she was. Quickly, I rose to my feet and undressed. Then, taking my wife by the hand, I led her to the hot tub and assisted her into the steaming water. The tub was chest deep, and her breasts floated on the surface of the water, her nipples pointing erotically toward me.

The waiters had opened a bottle of champagne and left it in an ice bucket with two delicate crystal flutes by the side of the tub. Reaching for the bottle, I poured champagne into the flutes, handing one to Yvette. "To another twenty-five blissful years," I said, touching our glasses together and sipping with her.

"You look more beautiful than ever," I added, feeling the heated water bubbling around and between our naked bodies. This time when we kissed, she pressed herself against me. I felt the points of her nipples burning into my bare chest like smoldering embers and her hand searching between us for my hardness. We stood that way for a long while, kissing and stroking each other in the enveloping comfort of the heated water.

Her hand glided lovingly over the throbbing rigidity of my manhood. The combination of her touch and the bubbles bursting against my naked skin lifted me to a state of pulsating excitement. I stroked her belly, moving my hand purposefully lower until my fingers encountered the wet fur of her pubis. Below the dense and curling triangle, her opening was moist. I slipped a finger inside, thrilled to find even more moisture within.

Taking advantage of the buoyancy, she gracefully lifted her body and wrapped her legs around my hips. My erection stood up to search for her feminine opening, relishing the heated liquid that swirled and bubbled around it. I placed my hands on her waist, guiding her slowly downward until she was poised just above the tip of my throbbing member.

With a sigh, she lowered herself onto me, burying my hardness in her tunnel by tantalizing degrees until I was deep inside the warmth of her womanhood. Gradually, almost imperceptibly, she ascended my staff, riding so high that for a moment I feared that the penetration would end. Then, reaching the pinnacle, she descended again, enveloping my pulsating flesh within her.

Unconsciously, we thrust in rhythm to the sound of waves crashing against the coastline. The moon shone on our writhing bodies, lighting the water that roiled around us and making us feel as though we were standing in the sea itself. We were both moved by the beauty of the moment, but even more by the rising excitement within our pounding loins. Without warning, my climax began. Then, as if cued by an unseen conductor, Yvette joined me. Together, we told the moon and the stars of the glory of our union.

Even after the spasms of ecstasy were spent, we remained tangled in each other's arms, bathing in the fluid of desire. I became hard again within minutes. When she felt my erection bumping demandingly against her, she hummed her approval. "Henry," she said adoringly. "You've got the sexual energy of a teenager. Take me again. Oh, yes, take me again."

Lifting her in my arms, I stepped up and out of the tub. With a strength that I had forgotten, I carried her, dripping, across the room to the immense platform bed and laid her gently down on the sheet. She moaned and reached for me, encircling my neck in her loving arms.

I lowered my naked body onto her, my questing rod instantly finding its mark. As I slipped inside her, I pressed our bodies together, reveling in the sensuous softness of her breasts against my wet skin.

THE BEST SEX I EVER HAD

We moved together for a long time, rising slowly to the peak of erotic pleasure and retreating deliberately to prolong the delight. Finally, when we could not draw our desperate contact out any longer, we came in unison, rolling and writhing in each other's arms like young lovers.

Afterward, we lay side by side in the night, enjoying the moonlit ocean view and fondling each other adoringly. Some time in the wee hours, we made love again, this time lazily and casually, celebrating the years we had spent learning about each other's bodies, demonstrating our ability to please each other's fancy and to satisfy each other's needs. When the sun rose, we did it again, welcoming the new day as the beginning of our second quarter-century together.

I'm still drilling teeth for a living. And there are still some evenings when I don't feel like doing anything but sit in front of the television set with Yvette by my side. But we seem to have rediscovered the ecstasy of romantic sex. That anniversary trip was an erotic rebirth for us, inspiring us to relive the passionate excitement that brought us together in the first place. We talk about it sometimes, whispering in our bed as we begin our lovemaking.

At our age it's rather difficult to select a single experience and call it the ultimate. But, without a doubt, that erotic holiday at the honeymoon cottage ranks with the best sex we ever had.

CONCLUSION

Everyone is looking for the secret of good sex, as if there were some magical, mechanical formula that leads to greater erotic delight. But the secret of sexual success is that there is no one secret. Good sex does not result simply from properly combining sex organs or from putting fingers and tongues in precisely the right places. It is not just a matter of nibbling the hot spot or learning to prolong intercourse for a specified number of hours.

The factors that make sex good, and that make good sex even better, exist in elusive combination. This combination varies from one couple to another. Some of these factors are so commonplace that they sound corny—candlelight and soft music, for example. Others are effective because they are unusual, like the special excitement some people get from making love in public places.

We conceived of this book when we realized that by looking at the sex that other people described as the best they ever had, we could learn ways of improving our own. Instead of trying to tell you how to have great sex, we decided to show you what worked for others. And that's what we've done. To protect our informants from embarrassment, we changed a few names and places. To make reading easier and more comfortable, we changed a phrase or two. For the most part, though, we have presented the recollections that real people have about their favorite sex experiences.

Our goal was to provide you with exciting ideas for enhancing your own erotic life so that every time you make love, you will feel like saying, "That was the best sex I ever had." We've done our job. The rest is up to you.

ATTENTION READERS:

The authors have already begun gathering information for their next book. If you would like to participate by filling out a questionnaire, please send your name and address to:

Steven and Iris Finz
1050 University Avenue (Ste 103)
San Diego, CA 92103

Your identity will be kept confidential.

- Should women draw a line between love and sex?

- When are fantasies harmful—and when are they helpful?

- Is "sex addiction" truly a sickness?

Bakos answers these and other questions with prescriptive advice that any woman can use to enjoy fulfilling sex and lasting relationships. In the author's singularly personal style, and in the words of hundreds of women from around the US, *Sexual Pleasures* brings wisdom, comfort, and sound counsel to women, *from* women.

SEXUAL PLEASURES
What Women Really Want,
What Women Really Need

SUSAN CRAIN BAKOS